Salad Cookbook 2022

....

....

....

....

300+ Recipes for Healthy and Simple Salads A New Cookbook for Colorful Dishes Using Veggies, Grains, Proteins, and More

....

....

....

....

D1245202

Alice A. Smith

TABLE OF CONTENTS

INTRODUCTIONS

RECIPE

Salad is a general term for a wide range of dishes, such as green salads, vegetable salads, salads made with pasta, beans, or grains, mixed salads with meat, poultry, or seafood, and fruit salads. Most salads are served cold, but some, like German potato salad, are traditionally served hot.

Since ancient times, people have known that green salad is good for you. "Eat cress and get smarter," says a Greek proverb. The first salads were made with wild greens and herbs seasoned with salt. These were the first vegetable foods that could be found in the spring, and they were a good pick-me-up after a bland winter diet. Green salads are eaten at the start of a meal, with the appetizer, or after the main dish. All types of lettuce, garden cress, watercress, endives, cabbage, spinach, escarole, romaine (cos), arugula, and fresh herbs are used. The green salad can be topped with raw or cooked vegetables like tomatoes, onions, cucumbers, peppers, beets, and so on. In France, a coupon is a piece of dry bread rubbed with garlic and added to a salad to add flavor. Caesar salad was first made in the 1920s in Tijuana, Mexico. It is a green salad made with romaine lettuce and a dressing made of crushed anchovies, olive oil, lemon juice, egg, and Parmesan cheese. Croutons are used as a garnish.

Vegetable salads can be made of raw or cooked vegetables that have been marinated or put in a sauce. Most of the time, tomatoes, green beans, cucumbers, beets, and mushrooms are the main ingredients. Cole slaw is made of shredded or chopped cabbage with mayonnaise or vinegar-based dressing. The name comes from the Dutch word for cabbage, kool. Middle Eastern salads are made with tahini or yogurt and finely chopped cucumbers, eggplants, or chickpeas. Salade Russe is a mix of cooked vegetables and potatoes that have been chopped up and held together with mayonnaise. Even though these salads are sometimes served as appetizers, they usually replace hot or cold vegetable sides. Rice, pasta, potatoes, dried beans, bulgur (cracked wheat), and other starches can be used to make salads that do the same thing. Mixed salads are heartier versions of salads with greens, vegetables, and grains. When you add meat, poultry, seafood, eggs, or cheese to a dish, it becomes a light main course. In the US, julienne salad is a green salad with thin strips of cheese, chicken, ham, beef, and vegetables. In France, salade Nicoise is made with lettuce, potatoes, green beans, olives, tuna, tomatoes, anchovies, and olive oil and vinegar. A Scandinavian specialty is a herring salad made with finely chopped pickled herring, potatoes, beetroot, cold meats like tongue or roast veal, onions, and apples.

People often eat desserts that are fruit salads with sweet dressings. Fruits can be added to green salads, and avocado, orange, and grapefruit go well with duck or pork, which are both fatty meats. The Waldorf salad is made with apples, walnuts, and celery mixed with mayonnaise. It is named after the Waldorf Hotel in New York City. Gelatins are often added to salads made of fruit or vegetables.

The simplest salad dressings are made from oil and vinegar (usually three parts oil to one part vinegar). Salt, pepper, herbs, and often Dijon mustard is added to this mixture. In France, the dressing sometimes gets a spoonful of the juices from a roast. Creamy dressings are made with mayonnaise, sweet or sour cream, or a sauce made with eggs, flour, milk, or cream that has been cooked. Green goddess dressing has green onions, garlic, anchovy paste, tarragon, and parsley. Thousand Island dressing has ketchup, minced onion, olives, onion, parsley, and an egg. The commercial "French" dressing used a lot in the United States is a mixture of tomato and vinegar that tastes sweet and sour.

HEALTHY SALAD NIÇOISE

Prep:15 mins

Cook:10 mins

Ingredients

- 200g new potato, thickly sliced
- 2 medium eggs
- 100g green bean, trimmed
- One romaine lettuce heart leaves separated and washed
- 8 cherry tomatoes, halved
- Six anchovies in olive oil drained well
- 197g can tuna steak in spring water, drained
- 2 tbsp reduced-fat mayonnaise

Method

STEP 1:

Boil a lot of water in a large pot—Cook for 7 minutes after adding the potatoes and eggs. Take the eggs out of the pan and add the green beans. Cook for four more minutes. Use a colander to drain the potatoes, beans, and eggs until they are excellent. Let things dry.

STEP 2

Peel the eggs and slice them in half. Set the lettuce leaves in the bottom of two shallow bowls. Spread the beans, potatoes, tomatoes, and egg quarters over the top. Use kitchen paper to soak up the extra oil from the anchovies, then put them on top.

STEP 3

Break the tuna into pieces and sprinkle them all over the salad. In a bowl, mix the mayonnaise and 1 tbsp of cold water until smooth. Pour the dressing over the salad, and serve.

GIANT COUSCOUS SALAD WITH CHARRED VEG & TANGY PESTO

Prep:25 mins

Cook:50 mins

Ingredients

- 2-3 raw beetroot (320g), peeled and chopped
- Three red onions (320g), cut into wedges
- Two green or orange peppers, deseeded and cubed
- 1 tbsp olive oil
- 320g cherry tomatoes
- 200g wholewheat giant couscous

For the pesto

- 7g fresh coriander, roughly chopped
- 15g flat-leaf parsley, roughly chopped
- 1 garlic clove
- One green chili, deseeded
- ½ tsp cumin
- 1 tbsp apple cider vinegar
- 1 tbsp olive oil
- 40g pine nuts, lightly toasted

Method
STEP 1

Heat the oven to 200C/180C fan/gas 6. In a bowl, toss the beetroot, onions, and peppers together with the oil, then spread out on a large roasting tray lined with baking paper and roast for 35 mins. Scatter over the cherry tomatoes, then return to the oven for 10 mins more until the tomatoes have softened and the vegetables are tender.

STEP 2

Meanwhile, cook the couscous following pack instructions, then rinse and drain. To make the pesto, put the coriander and half the parsley in a bowl with the garlic, chili, cumin, vinegar, oil, and 25g of pine nuts. Add 2 tbsp water, then blitz with a hand blender until smooth, or use a small food processor.

STEP 3

Toss the roasted veg and chopped parsley through the couscous and pile on the pesto, then scatter with the remaining pine nuts. If you're following the Healthy Diet Plan, serve half of the salad immediately, then chill the rest for another day.

BEETROOT & HALLOUMI SALAD WITH POMEGRANATE AND DILL

Prep:15 mins

Cook:1 min - 2 mins

Ingredients

- One medium red onion halved and thinly sliced
- 2 tbsp apple cider vinegar
- Two oranges

- Four handfuls of rocket leaves
- Two cooked beetroots, chopped
- drop rapeseed oil, for frying
- 80g thinly sliced halloumi, slices halved
- 80g pomegranate seeds
- 2 tbsp pumpkin seeds
- handful mint leaves
- few sprigs of dill, chopped

Method
STEP 1

Put the sliced onion in a bowl, add the vinegar, and mix well. Peel and core the orange, then cut it into segments over the onion bowl to catch any juice.

STEP 2

Spread the beetroot and orange slices over the rocket. Rub a drop of oil all over a nonstick frying pan, then fry the halloumi for about 30 seconds on every side, until golden.

STEP 3

Mix the pomegranate seeds into the onions, then pour the pomegranate mixture and the rest of the dressing over the rocket. Add the halloumi and sprinkle the pumpkin seeds, mint, and dill on top.

GREEN GODDESS SALAD

Ingredients
- Two heads of fennel, finely shaved
- 4 Baby Gem lettuces, cut into wedges
- One cucumber, cut into finger-size batons
- One bunch of spring onion, cut into finger-size batons

For the dressing

- 1 tbsp Dijon mustard
- 2 tbsp red wine vinegar
- 6 tbsp olive oil

Method
STEP 1

Put the ingredients for the dressing and a splash of water in a jar and shake it well.

STEP 2

Put the salad in a bowl and put it in the fridge for up to a day. Dress the salad before you serve it.

TURKEY, STRAWBERRY & AVOCADO SALAD

Prep:15 mins

Cook:10 mins

Ingredients

- 400g turkey breast mini fillets
- Two lemons, 1 zested and juiced, one sliced
- Three garlic cloves, crushed
- 1 tbsp maple syrup
- 2 tsp olive oil
- ½ tsp poppy seeds
- 160g baby spinach
- One avocado, peeled, stoned, and sliced
- 200g strawberries, hulled and cut into quarters
- 10g basil, torn

Method
STEP 1

Put the turkey fillets between two pieces of baking paper and roll them out with a rolling pin until they are 1 cm thick. Put the turkey, lemon slices, garlic, and 1 tsp salt in a large, deep pan. Cover the turkey with enough water to cover it, then bring to a boil over medium heat. Turn the heat down to low to medium, cover, and cook for 10 minutes, or until the turkey is cooked through and the juices run clear. Using a slotted spoon, move to a plate, loosely cover with foil, and set aside to cool a bit.

STEP 2

Mix the lemon juice and zest into the maple syrup. Whisk in the oil slowly, and then add the poppy seeds. Season.

STEP 3

Use two forks to shred the turkey. On every plate, put the turkey on top of the spinach, avocado, strawberries, and basil. Pour the dressing on to taste, and then serve.

HALLOUMI, CARROT & ORANGE SALAD

Prep:5 mins

Cook:15 mins

Ingredients

- Two large oranges
- 1½ tbsp wholegrain mustard
- 1½ tsp honey
- 1 tbsp white wine vinegar
- 3 tbsp rapeseed
- Two large carrots, peeled

- 225g block halloumi, sliced
- 100g bag watercress

Method
STEP 1

Cut the oranges peels and centers out. Use a small knife with a serrated edge to cut the orange into sections, catching the juices in a bowl. Squeeze any extra liquid from the pith into the bowl as well. Mix the mustard, honey, vinegar, oil, and seasonings in the bowl.

STEP 2

With a vegetable peeler, make carrot ribbons and put them in the bowl with the dressing. In a frying pan, heat a little bit of oil and cook the halloumi for a few minutes, until both sides are golden. Mix the watercress in with the carrots that have been dressed. Put the watercress mixture on plates, then add the halloumi and oranges.

QUINOA WITH ROAST ASPARAGUS, EGGS & CAPERS

Prep:20 mins

Cook:30 mins

Ingredients
- 1 tsp olive oil
- 500g asparagus (2 bunches), ends trimmed if tough and halved if very long
- Three courgettes (about 500g), thickly sliced
- Two red onions halved, then cut into chunks
- 150g quinoa
- Four eggs
- 400g can borlotti beans, drained

- Two ready-cooked beetroots (about 200g), diced

For the dressing

- 3 tbsp extra virgin olive oil
- 1 tbsp balsamic vinegar
- 4 tbsp chopped dill
- 1 tbsp capers

Method
STEP 1

Preheat the oven to 200C/180C fan/gas 6. Rub the oil on your hands, and then use them to toss and coat the asparagus, courgettes, and onions (you shouldn't need more than 1 tsp oil). Spread the vegetables out on two baking sheets and roast them for 20 to 25 minutes, or until they are soft and starting to turn color.

STEP 2

While that is going on, boil the quinoa in a lot of water for 20 minutes or until it is soft. Wait 5 minutes, then drain well and pour into a big bowl. Boil the eggs in another pan for 7 minutes. Run the eggs under cold water, remove the shells, and cut them in half.

STEP 3

Mix the olive oil, vinegar, 3 tbsp of the dill, and the capers to make the dressing. Add half of the beans, roasted courgettes, and onions to the quinoa. Mix well, then pile on a platter and top with the asparagus and egg halves. Spread over the beetroot, but try not to get the eggs stained pink. Mix in the remaining dressing and dill. Serve half and put the rest in the fridge for later. You can eat the leftovers cold, or you can heat them in the microwave or oven until they are hot all the way through. Covered and kept cool for two days.

COUSCOUS SALAD

Prep:10 mins

Serves 2

Ingredients

- 100g couscous
- 200ml hot low salt vegetable stock (from a cube is fine)
- Two spring onions
- One red pepper
- ½ cucumber
- 50g feta cheese, cubed
- 2tbsp pesto
- 2tbsp pine nuts

Method
STEP 1

Pour the stock over the couscous in a large bowl. Cover and let sit for 10 minutes, or until the rice is fluffy and the stock has been absorbed. Slice the onion and pepper, and cut the cucumber into small pieces. Add these to the couscous, mix the pesto and feta with a fork, and then top with pine nuts.

QUINOA SALAD WITH SHREDDED GREENS & RAISINS
Ingredients

- 150g quinoa
- 3 tbsp balsamic vinegar
- 2 tbsp extra virgin olive oil
- 200g cavolo nero, shredded

- One red onion, finely chopped
- One green pepper, deseeded and chopped into small pieces
- 30g raisins
- Two small avocados, chopped
- 40g vegetarian feta

Method
STEP 1

Rinse the quinoa in a sieve under running water until the water runs clear. Then, cook the quinoa according to the directions on the package for 20 minutes. Let it sit for 5 minutes. Rinse again and press down in the sieve to drain well.

STEP 2

In the meantime, mix the vinegar and oil in a large bowl. Add the kale and massage it with your hands to soften it.

STEP 3

Mix well after adding the quinoa, onion, pepper, and raisins. Put half on every plate, sprinkle one chopped avocado on top, crumble half of the feta on top, and toss. The rest can stay cold in the fridge for up to three days. Put the rest of the avocado and feta on top, and then serve.

FETA, BEETROOT& POMEGRANATE SALAD
Ingredients

- 2 tsp rapeseed oil
- 1 tbsp pomegranate molasses
- pinch of ground cinnamon
- 1 tsp cumin seeds, toasted
- a squeeze of lemon juice

- a handful of parsley, finely chopped
- a handful of mint leaves, torn
- Two cooked beetroots, cut into thin wedges
- 30g feta, crumbled
- a handful of rocket leaves
- ½ romaine lettuce, torn into bite-sized pieces
- 20g pomegranate seeds

Method
STEP 1

Mix the oil, pomegranate molasses, cinnamon, cumin seeds, and lemon juice in a bowl. Add 1 tsp of water to loosen it up, then season it.

STEP 2

Add the herbs, beets, feta, rocket, and lettuce, and toss to coat the dressing. To serve, sprinkle over the pomegranate seeds.

GUACAMOLE & MANGO SALAD WITH BLACK BEANS

Cook:15 mins

Serves 2

Ingredients
- One lime, zested and juiced
- One small mango, stoned, peeled, and chopped
- One small avocado, stoned, peeled, and chopped
- 100g cherry tomatoes, halved
- One red chili, deseeded and chopped
- One red onion, chopped
- ½ small pack of coriander, chopped
- 400g can black beans, drained and rinsed

Method
STEP 1:

Put the lime zest and juice, mango, avocado, tomatoes, chili, and onion in a bowl. Mix in the coriander and beans.

THREE BEAN SALAD WITH MOZZARELLA

Prep:20 mins

Cook:10 mins

Ingredients

- 320g fine beans, ends trimmed and halved if large
- Four carrots (320g), cut into slim batons
- Two red onions, halved and sliced
- 400g can cannellini beans, drained
- 400g can red kidney beans, drained
- 320g mixed color baby tomatoes (ours were red, yellow, and orange), halved
- 15g basil leaves, roughly torn
- 120g vegetarian mozzarella, cut into cubes

For the dressing

- 2 tbsp extra virgin olive oil
- 1-2 tbsp balsamic vinegar
- Two garlic cloves, finely chopped
- ½-1 tsp dried oregano
- 1 tsp dried English mustard powder
- 15 pitted Kalamata olives (about 45g), sliced
- ½ tsp lemon zest and 2 tbsp juice

Method
STEP 1

Boil or steam the green beans and carrots for 8 to 10 minutes, or until they are tender. Slice the onions and put them in a bowl. Pour boiling water over the onions until they are just covered.

STEP 2

In the meantime, make the sauce. In a large bowl, mix all the ingredients.

STEP 3

Pour the cooked beans and carrots into the dressing along with the drained onions, canned beans, and tomatoes. Toss well, then add the basil and toss again. Sprinkle the mozzarella on top and, if you like, grind some black pepper on top. It will stay cool for up to 3 days.

CHICKEN SHAWARMA SALAD

Prep:30 mins

Cook:10 mins

Ingredients

- Four garlic cloves, crushed
- 3 tbsp olive oil
- One lemon, juiced
- 2 tsp ground cumin
- 2 tsp ground coriander
- 2 tsp smoked paprika
- ½ tsp ground cinnamon
- ½ tsp chili powder
- 1 tsp dried oregano

- 1 tbsp natural yogurt
- Four chicken breasts, bashed with a rolling pin until slightly flattened
- pittas or flatbreads and pickled chilies

For the tahini dressing

- 2 tbsp tahini
- 1 lemon, juiced
- 200g natural yogurt
- 1 tsp whole cumin seeds

For the salad

- ½ red cabbage (about 500g), finely shredded
- Two red onions, finely sliced
- One small cucumber, peeled, halved, deseeded, and sliced
- 200g cherry tomatoes, halved
- 1 Little Gem lettuce, chopped
- One lemon, juiced
- 2 tbsp olive oil

Method
STEP 1

Mix the garlic, olive oil, and lemon juice in a plastic bowl or container that can be used again. Stir in all the spices, the oregano, a large pinch of salt, and the yogurt. Mix to make a paste. Put the chicken in and toss it around to coat it. Cover and let it marinate for at least an hour, or put it in the fridge overnight.

STEP 2

To make the dressing, put all the ingredients in a small bowl, mix well, season, cover, and put in the fridge until you're ready to use it. You can make it up to two days in advance. Mix everything in the salad except the lemon juice and olive oil. The salad can be put together 1 to 2 hours ahead of time and kept cold.

STEP 3

Start the grill or put a griddle pan on high heat. Cook the chicken that has been marinated for 5 minutes on every side, or until it has a light char and is fully cooked. Put down on a board and lift.

STEP 4

Pour the lemon juice and olive oil over the salad and sprinkle with salt. Toss everything together. Spread the salad on a big plate or pour it into a big serving bowl. Slice the chicken and arrange it on top of the salad. If you're also cooking for vegetarians, you can serve the chicken on the side. Serve the salad with the tahini dressing on the side, along with toasted flatbreads or pitas to put the chicken in and pickled chilies, if you like.

PORK SOUVLAKI WITH GREEK SALAD & RICE

Prep:15 mins

Cook:35 mins

Ingredients

- One garlic clove, finely grated
- 4 tsp olive oil
- ½ lemon, zested and juiced
- ¾ tsp dried oregano
- 250g lean pork tenderloin, cut into chunks
- One onion, finely chopped
- 85g brown basmati rice
- ½ tsp dried mint

- 1 tsp vegetable bouillon powder
- 2 tbsp chopped fresh dill
- 3 tomatoes, chopped
- 10cm chunk of cucumber, chopped
- 1 red onion, halved and thinly sliced
- 4 Kalamata olives, halved
- 1 tsp red wine vinegar
- 25g feta, crumbled

Method
STEP 1

In a large bowl, mix the garlic with 2 tsp of the oil, the lemon zest and 1 tsp of lemon juice, a lot of black pepper, and 12 tsp of oregano. Add the pork and stir it around so that it is well coated. If you have 30 minutes, set the meat aside to marinate.

STEP 2

Heat 1 tsp of olive oil in a pan that doesn't stick. Add the chopped onion, cover, and let it cook for 5 minutes. After that, remove the lid and stir in the rice, dried mint, and bouillon. Pour in 300ml boiling water. Cover and cook for 30–35 minutes, or until the rice is soft and the liquid has been absorbed. Add the dill and a squeeze of lemon juice, and mix well.

STEP 3

In the meantime, turn up the heat on the grill or start your barbecue. The pork should be put on two skewers. Mix the remaining oregano, vinegar, oil, and a squeeze of lemon with the tomatoes, cucumbers, red onions, and olives in a bowl. Put on plates, and then put feta on top.

STEP 4

For about 4 minutes on every side, grill the souvlaki until they are cooked but still juicy. Serve with rice and salad.

WILD SALMON WITH RADISH & ORANGE SLAW

Prep:25 mins

Cook:15 mins

Ingredients

- ½ tsp smoked paprika
- ½ tsp cumin seeds
- ¼ tsp ground cinnamon
- ¼ tsp orange zest
- Four wild salmon fillets (140g each)

For the radish slaw

- 600g baby potatoes
- Two red peppers halved and deseeded
- 1-2 green chilies, deseeded and finely chopped
- 1½ tbsp extra virgin olive oil
- 2 tbsp lemon juice
- 2 tbsp lemon zest
- 4 spring onions, finely sliced
- 320g radishes, thinly sliced
- 12 Kalamata olives, quartered
- Two small oranges, peeled and chopped
- 5 tbsp chopped mint

Method
STEP 1

Mix the paprika, cumin seeds, cinnamon, and orange zest, then rub the mixture all over the salmon fillets.

STEP 2

Boil the baby potatoes for 15 minutes with their skins until they are soft. Drain, then cut into thick pieces.

STEP 3

Heat the grill to high and grill the peppers for 5 minutes on every side, or until they are cooked through and charred. Peel off the blistered skins and cut the flesh into small pieces. Add the sliced potatoes, spring onions, radishes, olive oil, lemon juice and zest, and lemon zest to a bowl.

STEP 4

Cook the salmon with the skin side up for 5 minutes under the grill, then flip. If it's not already done, grill it for 1–2 more.

STEP 5

Mix the chopped olives, orange, and mint into the potatoes, and serve half of the potatoes with half of the salmon. Keep the rest in the fridge until another day. It will stay cool for up to two days if it is covered and kept cold.

GRILLED NECTARINE & BURRATA SALAD

Prep:10 mins

Cook:10 mins

Ingredients

- 15g unsalted butter

- 2 tbsp caster sugar
- 50g whole pecans
- Three ripe nectarines were stoned and cut into eighth lengthways
- 4 tbsp extra virgin olive oil, +extra for brushing
- 2 tbsp balsamic vinegar
- 1 tsp honey
- 2 x 100g balls of burrata or vegetarian alternative
- 70g rocket
- bunch of basil leaves, roughly torn
- pinch of chili flakes

Method
STEP 1

Melt the butter and sugar in a small frying pan over medium heat. Stir the pecans around in the buttery sugar to coat them. Keep cooking and stirring for about 5 minutes until the pecans are crisp and have a caramelized flavor. Pour the mixture out onto a piece of baking paper and let it cool. Once it has cooled, chop it roughly and set it aside.

STEP 2

Put a griddle pan over high heat and use a lot of olive oil to coat the nectarine slices. Griddle for 1–2 minutes on every side until browned and sticky. Put on a serving dish and set aside.

STEP 3

Mix the 4 tbsp of olive oil, vinegar, honey, and seasonings in a bowl. This will make a dressing.

STEP 4

Put the burrata balls in between the nectarines and cut them in half. Then put the rocket and basil around them. Pour the dressing over the salad, sprinkle with pecans, and add a pinch of chili flakes to serve.

ROASTED NEW POTATO, KALE & FETA SALAD WITH AVOCADO

Prep:15 mins

Cook:35 mins

Ingredients

- 200g Jersey Royal potatoes, halved
- Two garlic cloves
- 2 tbsp cold-pressed rapeseed oil
- One lemon, juiced
- One banana shallot, chopped
- 200g bag kale
- One small ripe avocado, flesh scooped out
- ½ tsp Dijon mustard
- 25g feta (or vegetarian alternative), crumbled
- ½-1 tsp chili flakes
- 1 tbsp pumpkin seeds, toasted

Method
STEP 1

Preheat oven to 200C/180C fan/gas 6. Boil the potatoes for 10 minutes or until they are mostly soft. Drain them and let them dry in the steam. Put the potatoes and garlic in a large roasting pan. Drizzle with 1 tbsp of oil and season with salt and pepper. For 20 minutes, roast.

STEP 2

While the potatoes are roasting, squeeze half the lemon juice over the shallot and half of the kale, season, and then massage gently to soften the kale.

STEP 3

Take the cloves of garlic out of the oven. Put the rest of the kale on top of the potatoes, drizzle a little oil on top, sprinkle with salt, and put back in the oven for 5 minutes until the kale is crisp.

STEP 4

In the meantime, blend the garlic, avocado, mustard, the rest of the oil, the lemon juice, and enough water to make a smooth dressing. Mix the potatoes and cooked kale into the raw kale salad and put it on a platter. Pour the sauce over the salad, then sprinkle the feta, chili flakes, and pumpkin seeds.

QUICK CHICKEN HUMMUS BOWL

Prep:10 mins

Serves 2

Ingredients

- 200g hummus
- One small lemon, zested and juiced
- 200g pouch cooked mixed grains
- 150g baby spinach, roughly chopped
- 1 small avocado, halved and sliced
- 1cooked chicken breast, cut at an angle
- 100g pomegranate seeds
- ½ red onion, finely sliced
- 2 tbsp toasted almonds

Method
STEP 1

Mix 2 tbsp of the hummus, half of the lemon juice, the lemon zest, and enough water to make a dressing that can be drizzled. Squeeze the grain pouch to get the grains out, then put them in two shallow bowls and pour the sauce over them. Add a handful of spinach to every bowl.

STEP 2

Squeeze the rest of the lemon juice over the avocado halves, then put one half in every bowl. Before eating, divide the chicken, pomegranate seeds, onion, almonds, and the rest of the hummus between the two bowls and gently mix everything.

SHAVED FENNEL & ROCKET SALAD

Prep:5 mins

Serves 4

Ingredients

- One fennel bulb
- 1/2 tsp fennel seeds
- 1/2 lemon, juiced
- 2 tbsp olive oil
- 50g rocket

Method
STEP 1

Take the leaves off the fennel bulb and set them aside. Cut off tough stalks, then use a sharp knife or, better yet, a mandoline to slice the bulb into thin slices. Put the fennel slices in a bowl and mix in a large pinch of salt, the fennel seeds, if you're using them, and the lemon juice with your hands. Cover and let stand at room temperature for at least 10 minutes, or put in the fridge for up to a few hours.

STEP 2

Pour the olive oil over the pickled fennel, toss it with the rocket, and the fennel fronds you saved. You can serve it right out of the bowl or pile it on plates.

CURRIED PORK BULGUR SALAD

Prep:5 mins

Cook:8 mins

Ingredients

- 50g bulgur wheat
- 1 tsp Madras curry powder
- ¼ tsp cumin seeds
- 1 tsp vegetable bouillon
- Two Medjool dates, sliced
- Three spring onions, sliced
- 4 tsp chopped mint
- a handful of coriander, chopped
- ¼ cucumber, diced
- Two tomatoes, cut into wedges
- 120g leftover cooked pork, chopped
- ½ lemon, cut into wedges

Method
STEP 1

Put the bulgur, curry powder, cumin seeds (if using), bouillon, dates, and spring onions into a small pan. Pour 300 ml of boiling water over the bulgur and cook, covered, for 5 to 8 minutes, or until the liquid is absorbed and the bulgur is soft. Let it cool down all the way.

STEP 2

Mix in the pork, cucumber, tomatoes, mint, and coriander. Place in containers and top with lemon wedges. Just before eating, squeeze the lemon wedges over the salad and mix it in. It will stay good in the fridge for two to three days.

ROASTED ASPARAGUS & PEA SALAD

Prep:10 mins

Cook:10 mins

Ingredients

- 3 tbsp natural yogurt
- 1 tsp wholegrain mustard
- ½ tsp honey
- ½ lemon, zested and juiced
- 100g watercress
- One large slice of sourdough bread
- 200g asparagus, tough ends removed
- 1 ½ tbsp cold-pressed rapeseed oil
- 2 eggs
- 200g frozen peas

Method
STEP 1

Preheat the oven to 220C/200C fan/gas 7. Mix the yogurt, mustard, and honey. Add the lemon zest, then add the lemon juice and seasonings to taste. Any extra lemon juice should be squeezed over the watercress.

STEP 2

Tear the bread into rough pieces and put them and the asparagus on a large roasting tray. Toss the asparagus and croutons in the rapeseed oil and seasonings. Roast for 10 minutes, or until the asparagus is soft and the croutons are golden.

STEP 3

In the meantime, cook the eggs for 6 minutes in a pan of boiling water. Then, add the frozen peas and cook for one more minute. Drain both and rinse them in cold water until they are excellent. Peel the eggs and cut them in half.

STEP 4

To put the salad together, mix the asparagus and peas with the watercress. Then, add the creamy dressing and toss. Place the eggs and croutons in the bowl and serve.

COD WITH CUCUMBER, AVOCADO & MANGO SALSA SALAD

Prep:5 mins

Cook:8 mins

Ingredients

- 2 x skinless cod fillets
- One lime, zested and juiced
- One small mango, peeled, stoned, and chopped
- One small avocado, stoned, peeled, and sliced
- ¼ cucumber, chopped
- 160g cherry tomatoes, quartered
- One red chili, deseeded and chopped

- Two spring onions, sliced
- handful chopped coriander

Method
STEP 1

Preheat oven to 200C/180C fan/gas 6. Put the fish in a shallow dish that can go in the range. Pour half of the lime juice over the fish, along with some of the lime zest, and then grind some black pepper on top. Bake the fish for 8 minutes, or until it is flaky but still moist.

STEP 2

In the meantime, mix the remaining lime juice and zest with the rest of the ingredients in a bowl. Put some sauce on every plate, then add the cod and juices from the dish.

CHICKPEA SALAD

Prep:10 mins

Serves 6

Ingredients
- 400g can chickpeas, drained and rinsed
- small pack coriander, roughly chopped
- small pack parsley, roughly chopped
- One red onion, thinly sliced
- Two large tomatoes, chopped
- 2 tbsp olive oil
- 2 tbsp harissa
- One lemon, juiced

Method
STEP 1

Mix all the ingredients, mashing some of the chickpeas so that the edges are a little rough. This helps the chickpeas soak up the dressing. (It can be made a day ahead and kept in the fridge.) Try it with tzatziki sauce and slow-cooked Greek lamb.

GRILLED COURGETTE & HALLOUMI SALAD WITH CAPER & LEMON DRESSING

Prep:10 mins

Cook:20 mins

Ingredients

- 10-12 baby courgettes, halved lengthways
- 1 tbsp olive oil
- 225g block halloumi, thinly sliced (about 16 slices)

For the dressing

- One long shallot, finely chopped
- One red chili, finely chopped
- One garlic clove, crushed
- One lemon, zested and juiced
- 2 tbsp capers
- 3 tbsp olive oil

Method
STEP 1

Mix all dressing ingredients with 1 tbsp of cold water and a pinch of salt in a bowl. Mix and set aside.

STEP 2

Pour the oil over the courgettes in a large bowl. Add a little salt, and then mix.

STEP 3

Put the cut side of the courgettes down on a hot griddle pan. This is best done in batches. Cook for 4 to 5 minutes, until char marks appear and the meat softens, then flip and cook for another 3 minutes. Move to a shallow bowl and cover with foil to keep warm.

STEP 4

In the meantime, heat a large nonstick frying pan and put the halloumi in it. Wait a few minutes until both sides are golden brown.

STEP 5

Put the zucchini and halloumi on a large plate or platter, and then pour the dressing on top.

EPIC SUMMER SALAD

Prep:10 mins

Serves 6

Ingredients

- 400g black beans, drained
- Two large handfuls of baby spinach leaves, roughly chopped
- 500g heritage tomatoes, chopped into large chunks
- ½ cucumber halved lengthways, seeds scooped out and sliced at an angle
- One mango, peeled and chopped into chunks

- One large red onion halved and finely sliced
- 6-8 radishes, sliced
- Two avocados, peeled and sliced
- 100g feta, crumbled
- handful of herbs

For the dressing

- large bunch mint
- small bunch coriander
- small bunch basil
- One fat green chili, deseeded and chopped
- One small garlic clove
- 100ml extra virgin olive oil
- Two limes, zested and juiced
- 2 tbsp white wine vinegar
- 2 tsp honey

Method
STEP 1

Make the dressing by putting all ingredients in a food processor or chopping them very finely, leaving a few herb leaves for the salad. The sauce can be made up to 24 hours before it is served.

STEP 2

Spread the beans and spinach out on a big dish. Place the tomatoes, cucumber, mango, onion, and radishes on top, and then use your hands to gently mix everything. Avocados, feta, and herbs go on top of the salad, and the dressing is served on the side.

HEALTHY POTATO SALAD

Prep:10 mins

Cook:30 mins

Ingredients

- 1large bunch basil
- 1large bunch parsley
- 1kg new potatoes, larger potatoes halved
- 100ml extra virgin olive oil
- 2 tbsp white wine vinegar
- One small garlic clove

Method
STEP 1

Bring a large pot of salted water to a boil. Add the basil and let it cook for 30 seconds, or until it wilts. Take it out with a slotted spoon and set it aside to cool. Cook the potatoes until they are soft.

STEP 2

In the meantime, squeeze the basil over the sink and add the oil, vinegar, garlic, and a good pinch of seasoning to a blender. Blitz until you have a vibrant green oil.

STEP 3

Drain the potatoes and dry them with steam. Chop the parsley, and then put it and the potatoes in a bowl to serve. Add the basil oil and seasonings. Stays suitable for two days.

TACO SALAD

Prep:20 mins

Cook:30 mins

Ingredients

- One red onion, sliced
- One lime, juiced
- 1 tbsp sunflower oil
- 400g lean beef mince
- ½ pack taco or fajita seasoning
- 1 tbsp tomato purée
- 400g can black beans, drained but not rinsed
- 200g tortilla chips
- One small iceberg lettuce, shredded
- Two avocados, peeled and sliced
- Two tomatoes, chopped into chunks
- 100g feta, crumbled
- small bunch of coriander, chopped

For the dressing

- ½ lime, juiced
- 5 tbsp soured cream
- chili sauce +extra to serve

Method
STEP 1

In a small bowl, mix the red onion with half of the lime juice and a pinch of salt. Set aside.

STEP 2

Over medium-low heat, heat the oil in a frying pan and then crumble in the mince. Cook for 15 to 20 minutes. The meat will release some liquid, but once that has bubbled away, it will sizzle in its own fat. At this point, use a wooden spoon to stir or toss the mince around, so it browns and caramelizes all over. If the pan gets too dry, drizzle more oil into it. When the meat is nicely browned, sprinkle it with taco seasoning and let it cook for 2 minutes. Then, stir in the tomato purée, pour the rest of the lime juice on top, and let it sizzle for another minute. Add the black beans and stir them in. Raise the heat to be medium and keep cooking until everything is hot. Taste for seasoning, and then set aside.

STEP 3

To make the dressing, mix the lime juice with the sour cream and if you're using it, the chili sauce. Season with salt and pepper then set aside.

STEP 4

Put a handful of tortilla chips in a bowl, then a layer of lettuce, then a layer of mince, and then a layer of black beans. Put the avocado slices, chopped tomato, pickled red onions, along with any juices, and feta on top. Pour on the dressing, and then sprinkle on the coriander. Place more tortilla chips around the bowl's edges, and then serve.

CHOPPED GREEN SALAD WITH HERBY CHILLI DRESSING

Prep:15 mins

Serves 8

Ingredients
For the dressing

- zest and juice two lemons
- 4 tbsp extra virgin olive oil
- 1 tbsp white wine vinegar
- Two garlic cloves
- One green chili
- large handful of parsley leaves
- large handful of coriander leaves

For the salad

- Two cos or romaine lettuces, chopped
- Two avocados, stoned, peeled, and chopped
- ½ cucumber, sliced
- Two green peppers, deseeded and sliced
- Two celery sticks, sliced diagonally
- bunch spring onions, sliced diagonally

Method
STEP 1

Mix all the ingredients for the dressing with a stick blender or the small bowl of a food processor. How do you like it?

STEP 2

To serve, put all the salad ingredients in a large bowl, drizzle with the dressing, and toss.

SPRING TABBOULEH

Prep:20 mins

Cook:25 mins

Ingredients

- 6 tbsp olive oil
- 1 tbsp garam masala
- 2 x 400g cans chickpeas, drained and rinsed
- 250g ready-to-eat mixed grain pouch
- 250g frozen peas
- Two lemons, zested and juiced
- large pack parsley leaves roughly chopped
- a large pack of mint leaves roughly chopped
- 250g radishes, roughly chopped
- One cucumber, chopped
- pomegranate seeds, to serve

Method
STEP 1

Preheat oven to 200C/180C fan/gas 6. Mix the garam masala and some seasonings with 4 tbsp of oil. Mix with the chickpeas and put in a large roasting pan. Bake for 15 minutes or until the edges start to get crispy. Mix in the peas, lemon zest, and mixed grains. Mix well, and then put back in the oven for about 10 minutes, or until everything is warm.

STEP 2

Move to a large bowl or platter, then mix the herbs, radishes, cucumber, the rest of the oil, and the lemon juice. Season to your taste, then sprinkle the pomegranate seeds on top. You can eat any leftovers for lunch the next day.

LIME PRAWN COCKTAIL PITTA SALAD

Prep:10 mins

Cook:15 mins

Ingredients

- ½ wholemeal pitta
- ½ tbsp rapeseed oil
- 1 tsp Tabasco
- 1 tsp low-sugar, low-salt ketchup
- 1 tbsp low-fat mayonnaise
- 1 tbsp fat-free natural yogurt
- ½ lime, zested and juiced, +wedges to serve
- 60g cooked king prawns
- 1 Little Gem lettuce, leaves separated
- ¼ small cucumber, peeled into ribbons
- Four cherry tomatoes halved

Method
STEP 1

Preheat the oven to 200C/180C fan/gas 6. Put the pita triangles on a baking sheet and drizzle the oil over them. Bake for 10–15 minutes, or until golden and crisp.

STEP 2

Mix the Tabasco, ketchup, mayonnaise, yogurt, zest, and lime juice. Toss the shrimp in the sauce.

STEP 3

Put the lettuce, cucumber, tomatoes, and prawns dressed in a jar or lunchbox. Season, sprinkle the pita chips on top, and serve with wedges of lime.

SALMON SALAD WITH SESAME DRESSING

Prep:7 mins

Cook:16 mins

Ingredients
For the salad

- 250g new potatoes, sliced
- 160g French beans, trimmed
- Two wild salmon fillets
- 80g salad leaves
- Four small clementines, three sliced, one juiced
- a handful of basil, chopped
- a handful of coriander, chopped

For the dressing

- 2 tsp sesame oil
- 2 tsp tamari
- ½ lemon, juiced
- One red chili, deseeded and chopped
- 2 tbsp finely chopped onion

Method
STEP 1

Cook the potatoes and beans for 8 minutes in a steamer basket over boiling water. Place the salmon fillets on top and steam for another 6 to 8 minutes, or until a fork easily flakes the salmon.

STEP 2

Mix the ingredients for the dressing with the juice from the clementines. If you want to eat right away, put the salad leaves on two plates and put the warm potatoes, beans, and clementine slices on top. Place the salmon fillets on top, sprinkle the herbs over them, and pour the dressing on top. If you want to take it to work, make the potatoes, beans, and salmon the night before and put them in a rigid container with a tight lid. Keep the salad leaves separate. Put the salad together and dress it right before you eat it, so the leaves don't get soggy.

EGYPTIAN EGG SALAD

Prep:10 mins

Cook:5 mins

Ingredients

- Two large eggs
- One lemon, juiced
- 1 tbsp tahini
- 1 tbsp rapeseed oil
- One red onion, chopped
- 3 large garlic cloves, finely chopped
- 1 tsp ground cumin
- ½ tsp cumin seeds
- 400g can borlotti or fava beans, juice reserved
- 2 Little Gem lettuces cut into wedges
- Two tomatoes, cut into wedges
- a sprinkling of dried chili flakes and roughly chopped flat-leaf parsley,

Method
STEP 1

Bring a pan of water to a boil, put the eggs in, and let them boil for 8 minutes. Drain them and run them under cold water to cool them down a bit, then peel and cut them in half. To make a dressing, mix 1 tbsp of lemon juice and 3 tbsp of water with the tahini.

STEP 2

To soften the onion and garlic, heat the oil and fry them for 5 minutes. Add the ground cumin and seeds and stir briefly. Then add the beans and lightly crush some of them as you heat them. Add juice from the can to get a nice creamy texture, but leave some beans whole. Taste it and, if necessary, add a little lemon juice and some seasoning.

STEP 3

Put the beans and lettuce on plates, then add the eggs and tomatoes. If you want, you can also add the tahini dressing, chili, and parsley.

QUINOA SALAD WITH AVOCADO MAYO

Prep:10 mins

Cook:18 mins

Ingredients

- 70g quinoa
- 75g avocado, halved and stoned
- One small garlic clove, finely grated
- ½ tsp mustard powder
- One lemon, juiced and half zested
- 198g can sweetcorn, drained
- 160g cherry tomatoes, halved
- 2 x 5cm chunks of cucumber, diced
- Two spring onions, finely sliced
- 2 tbsp chopped mint
- 2 tbsp pumpkin seeds

- 100g cooked chicken

Method
STEP 1

Put the quinoa in a pot of boiling water and let it simmer for about 18 minutes, or until the grains pop. Pour into a sieve and run cold water over it.

STEP 2

In the meantime, put the avocado in a bowl, add the garlic, mustard, and 2 tbsp of lemon juice, and mash it all together with a hand blender or in a food processor until it's smooth. If it's too thick, add 1–2 tsp of cold water.

STEP 3

Mix the lemon zest, corn, salad vegetables, mint, and pumpkin seeds into the quinoa. Add a little more lemon juice to taste. Pour onto plates or into containers. If you're using chicken, put it on top, and then drizzle the avocado mayo on top.

BBQ RAINBOW BEEF SALAD

Prep:20 mins

Cook:6 mins

Ingredients
- 2 x 250g sirloin steaks, fat trimmed
- a thumb-sized piece of ginger, finely grated
- One garlic clove, finely grated
- Two limes, juiced
- 2 tbsp sesame oil
- 1 tbsp low-salt soy sauce

- Three red bird's eye chilies, two finely chopped, one finely sliced
- 4 Little Gem lettuces
- 12 radishes, thinly sliced
- Three carrots, peeled and finely sliced
- ½ cucumber, cut into ribbons using a peeler
- Three spring onions, finely sliced
- One large ripe avocado, sliced
- ½ tbsp mixed sesame seeds

Method
STEP 1

Take the steak out of the fridge an hour before you want to cook it so it can warm up. Before you start cooking, mix the ginger, garlic, lime juice, oil, soy sauce, and chopped chilies in a bowl.

STEP 2

Put the steaks on the grill and cook them for 3 minutes on one side, then flip them and cook for another 3 minutes on the other side for medium rare. You could also fry your steaks for 3 minutes on every side in a frying pan or griddle pan. Cover the meat for 5 minutes after it's done cooking.

STEP 3

Put the lettuce leaves, radishes, carrot, cucumber, spring onion, and avocado on a plate for everyone to share. Thinly slice the steak across the grain and put it on top of the salad. Drizzle the dressing and any juices that are left over on top. Add the sliced red chili and sesame seeds to the top.

SALADE NIÇOISE

Prep:20 mins

Cook:15 mins

Ingredients

- Eight new potatoes
- 50g green beans trimmed and halved
- Three eggs
- 2 Little Gem lettuces, quartered
- 50g pitted black olives
- Two medium tomatoes (plum are good), quartered
- 145g can tuna in olive oil, drained, oil reserved

For the dressing

- ½ garlic clove
- One anchovy fillet
- 1 tbsp Dijon mustard
- 2 tbsp red wine vinegar
- 4 tbsp reserved olive oil from the tuna can

Method
STEP 1

 To make the dressing, mash the garlic and anchovy if you're using it, with a pinch of salt on a board or in a pestle and mortar. Mix the mustard and vinegar into the paste, and then slowly stir in the tuna oil. Set aside.

STEP 2

Put the new potatoes in a large pan with cold, salted water and make sure they are completely covered. Bring to a boil, then turn the heat down to a slow spot. Add the beans and let them cook for 5 minutes. Take them out with a slotted spoon and put them in a bowl of iced water to cool down. Cook the potatoes for another 5 minutes, or until they are soft. Then drain them and set them aside to cool. When they are cool enough to handle, cut them in half or quarters and mix them with 1 tbsp of the dressing in a large bowl. Let it cool down all the way.

STEP 3

In the second pan of simmering water, cook the eggs for 7 1/2 minutes. Then, put them in a bowl of iced water to cool. Drain the beans and eggs, and then peel the eggs and cut them in half.

STEP 4

Put the lettuce quarters, beans that have been cooked, and olives in the bowl with the potatoes. Add most of the dressing that is left and toss gently. Put the salad in two bowls, then put the tomatoes and eggs on top. Sprinkle the tuna with the flakes, drizzle the rest of the dressing over it, and season.

QUINOA SALAD WITH EGGS & DILL

Prep:15 mins

Cook:30 mins

Ingredients

- 120g quinoa, rinsed
- Six eggs
- 320g asparagus, woody ends trimmed and halved if too long
- 4 tbsp extra virgin olive oil
- 2 tsp apple cider vinegar
- Six spring onions, finely chopped
- 2 tbsp chopped dill

- 2 tbsp chopped basil, +a few leaves to serve
- 15g capers, rinsed
- 320g cherry tomatoes, halved

Method
STEP 1

Boil the quinoa for 20 minutes in a lot of water. Leave for 5 minutes, then thoroughly rinse and drain. While the asparagus is steaming, boil the eggs for 7 minutes in a separate pan. If the eggs are done, but the asparagus is still not soft, take the eggs out of the pan and put them in a bowl of cold water while you cook the asparagus for a few more minutes. Separate the eggs.

STEP 2

To make the dressing, mix the chopped spring onions, herbs, and capers with the extra virgin olive oil and apple cider vinegar.

STEP 3

Put the quinoa in a bowl and toss it with the tomatoes and 3/4 of the dressing. Put half on plates and the other half in two containers. Set the asparagus on top of the salads and put three egg halves on everyone. Pour the rest of the dressing on top and sprinkle the basil leaves over the top. Close the bags and put them in the fridge. Will keep in the refrigerator for up to a day in a container with a lid.

PESTO CHICKEN SALAD

Prep:20 mins

Serves 2

Ingredients
- 50g couscous

- 2 tbsp pesto
- 2 tbsp fat-free yogurt
- Two cooked skinless chicken breasts, shredded, or 200g leftover roast chicken, shredded
- ½ small bunch of basil leaves picked and torn, and +a few small leaves to serve
- ½ cucumber, chopped
- Two sundried tomatoes in oil, drained and sliced
- 2 Little Gem lettuces, leaves separated
- 2 tsp toasted pine nuts

Method
STEP 1

Put 100ml of boiling water on top of the couscous in a large heat-safe bowl. Add 1 tbsp of pesto. Cover and wait 8 minutes.

STEP 2

Use a fork to fluff the couscous, then mix the rest of the pesto, the yogurt, and some seasonings. Put the chicken, basil, cucumber, and tomatoes into the bowl.

STEP 3

Spoon the couscous mixture into the lettuce leaves and eat with your fingers, or serve over the lettuce as a salad. Before you do, sprinkle the pine nuts and more basil on top.

SALMON PASTA SALAD WITH LEMON & CAPERS

Prep:10 mins

Cook:20 mins

Ingredients

- 85g wholewheat penne

- 1 tbsp rapeseed oil
- One large red pepper, roughly chopped
- Two frozen, skinless wild salmon fillets (about 120g each)
- One lemon, zested and juiced
- Two garlic cloves, finely grated
- One shallot, very finely chopped
- 2 tbsp capers
- 6 pitted Kalamata olives, sliced
- 1 tsp extra virgin olive oil
- Two handfuls rocket

Method
STEP 1

Cook the pasta by following the directions on the package. In the meantime, heat the rapeseed oil in a frying pan and add the pepper. Cover the pan and let it sit for about 5 minutes until the pepper softens and starts to get a little charred. Stir, then move the pepper to one side and add the salmon. Cover and cook for 8 to 10 minutes, or until almost done.

STEP 2

During this time, mix the lemon zest and juice with the garlic, shallot, capers, and olives in a large bowl.

STEP 3

Add the pepper and salmon that have been cooked to the bowl. Drain the pasta and add it to the mixture, along with the black pepper and olive oil. Mix everything while you break up the salmon. If you want to eat it right away, mix in the rocket. If you're going to pack it for lunch, let it cool, then put it in a container with the missile on top and mix it in right before you eat it.

SHREDDED CHARRED CORN SALAD

Prep:20 mins

Cook:10 mins

Ingredients

- ½ small white cabbage, finely shredded
- Two carrots, grated
- One red onion halved and finely sliced
- 3 tbsp cider vinegar
- 1 tsp caster sugar
- Four corn cobs
- 1 tbsp wholegrain mustard

Method
STEP 1

Put the cabbage, carrots, and onion in a bowl. Salt the food, then add the vinegar and sugar and mix everything. Leave the vegetables alone for 20 minutes so they can lightly pickle.

STEP 2

In the meantime, cook the corn on a hot grill or griddle pan for 4-5 minutes on every side, or until the kernels are darker and have a little bit of a char. Set aside to cool. Once the cobs are cool, stand them up on a board and use a sharp knife to cut the kernels off in long strips that go down.

STEP 3

Mix the mustard and half of the corn into the salad. Taste it to see if it needs more salt or pepper. Serve with the rest of the corn on top.

COURGETTI WITH CHILLI, LEMON, RICOTTA & MINT

Prep:15 mins

Serves 2

Ingredients

- Two courgettes (about 400g), ends trimmed and spiralized into thin noodles
- ½ red chili, thinly sliced
- zest and juice of ½ lemon
- ½ small pack of mint leaves picked
- 50g soft ricotta

Method
STEP 1

Mix the courgette, chili, lemon juice, 34 of the mint, flaky sea salt, and black pepper in a bowl. Place on a plate and decorate with lemon zest, the mint you saved, and small dollops of ricotta.

ROASTED SQUASH & RED ONION WITH PISTACHIOS

Prep:15 mins

Cook:25 mins

Ingredients

- One large butternut squash, peeled, ends trimmed, halved widthways, and spiralized into thick noodles
- One large red onion, peeled, ends cut, and spiralized using the ribbon attachment

- 2 tbsp olive oil
- 2 tsp sumac
- 50g pomegranate seeds
- 30g pistachios, toasted and roughly chopped

Method
STEP 1

Preheat oven to 200C/180C fan/gas 6. Mix the spiralized butternut squash and onion with the oil, sumac, some sea salt, and black pepper in a roasting tray. Spread out the vegetables and roast them for 25 minutes, or until they are completely soft and starting to caramelize.

STEP 2

Put some on every plate and sprinkle the pomegranate seeds and toasted pistachios on top.

SWEET MUSTARD POTATO SALAD

Prep:10 mins

Cook:10 mins

Ingredients
- 1.2kg waxy potatoes, such as Charlotte, cut into small chunks
- 400g good-quality mayonnaise
- 2 tbsp American mustard
- 2 tbsp cider vinegar
- 2 tbsp honey
- hard-boiled eggs, finely chopped
- Eight spring onions, sliced

Method
STEP 1

Put the potatoes in a pan with salted water, bring to a boil, cover, and cook on low heat for 8–10 minutes, or until a knife can quickly go through them. Drain and put in a colander to cool.

STEP 2

Mix the mayonnaise, mustard, vinegar, honey, and eggs together, then add the spices. Stir in the potatoes and half of the spring onions. Put the mixture on a serving dish and sprinkle the rest of the onions on top. Put in the fridge until it's time to serve. It can be made one day ahead.

CRUNCHY BULGUR SALAD

Prep:10 mins

Cook:15 mins

Ingredients

- 200g bulgur wheat
- 150g frozen edamame (podded)
- 2 Romano peppers, sliced into rounds, seeds removed
- 150g radishes, finely sliced
- 75g whole blanched almonds
- small bunch of mint, finely chopped
- small bunch of parsley, finely chopped
- Two oranges
- 3 tbsp olive oil

Method
STEP 1

Follow the directions on the package to cook the bulgur, then drain it and put it in a large serving bowl to cool. In the meantime, put the edamame beans in a small bowl, pour boiling water over them, and let them sit for 1 minute before draining. Mix with the peppers, radishes, almonds, mint, and parsley and put in a bowl to serve.

STEP 2

Peel one orange, cut the segments out with care, and add them to the bowl. Put the oil and the other fruit juice in a jam jar. Season it well and shake it to make it blend. If you're following our Healthy Diet Plan, divide the salad into four bowls or lunchboxes, pour half of the dressing on the two servings you'll eat today, and put the rest in the fridge for another day. The salad will last for two days in the refrigerator.

SALSA VERDE SALMON WITH SMASHED CHICKPEA SALAD

Prep:15 mins

Cook:20 mins

Ingredients

- 3 tsp olive oil
- One orange, zested and juiced
- Two skin-on salmon fillets
- small bunch of parsley (including stalks), finely chopped
- ½ tbsp Dijon mustard
- One shallot or 1/2 small red onion, finely chopped
- ½ tbsp red wine vinegar

- 400g can chickpeas, drained and rinsed
- Two roasted red peppers from a jar, drained and chopped
- 50g kale

Method

STEP 1

Put the grill on high heat. Mix the orange zest, a splash of orange juice, a lot of black pepper, and a pinch of salt with 1 tsp of the oil. Place the salmon, skin side down, on a baking sheet that won't stick, and pour the marinade over it. Make the salsa while you let the meat marinate at room temperature.

STEP 2

Put the parsley, mustard, half of the shallot, vinegar, 1 tsp oil, and the other orange juice in a small food processor and blend until you have a thick sauce. If you need to thin it out, add a splash of water.

STEP 3

In a frying pan, heat the rest of the oil and cook the remaining shallots for 5 minutes. Add the chickpeas and some seasoning, turn up the heat and stir until the chickpeas are just starting to crisp. Use a potato masher to break up the potatoes and mix the roasted peppers and kale. Add a splash of water and cover with a lid until the kale has wilted. Use low heat to keep warm.

STEP 4

Grill the salmon for four to six minutes, or until it's done the way you like. On a plate, put half of the chickpeas, a salmon fillet (leave the skin on if you want), and some of the salsa verde. Let the other salmon fillet cool down so you can put it in your lunchbox, see tip below.

GRILLED AUBERGINE TABBOULEH

Prep:15 mins

Cook:10 mins

Ingredients

- 2 tbsp garlic-infused oil
- 1 large aubergine , diced
- 160g couscous
- ½ cucumber, diced
- 200g cherry tomatoes, halved
- small pack mint, roughly chopped
- small pack parsley, roughly chopped

For the dressing

- juice one lemon
- 5 tbsp coconut yogurt
- 2 tbsp tahini
- 1 tbsp maple syrup

Method
STEP 1

Heat the oil in a skillet over medium-high heat, then add the eggplant. Cook for 10 minutes, or until soft and done.

STEP 2

In the meantime, pour 200ml of boiling water over the couscous in a large bowl. Cover with plastic wrap and let sit for 5–6 minutes. Mix all of the dressing's ingredients, and then add salt and pepper to taste.

STEP 3

When all the water has been soaked up by the couscous, fluff it up with a fork. Season the cucumber, tomatoes, and herbs, then mix them in. Mix in half of the sauce and toss to coat. Spread the rest of the dressing over the aubergine, and then serve.

BROCCOLI SALAD

Prep:10 mins

Cook:3 mins

Ingredients

- 300g broccoli florets, broken into small pieces
- Two carrots, peeled lengthways into large ribbons
- 50g dried cranberries
- 50g cashews, toasted, roughly chopped

For the pickle

- 80ml cider vinegar
- 1 tbsp caster sugar
- ¼ tsp sea salt flakes
- 1 red onion, finely sliced

For the dressing

- 50ml extra virgin olive oil
- 1 tbsp maple syrup
- One lemon, zested and juiced

Method
STEP 1

To make the pickle, heat the vinegar, sugar, and salt in a small pan. Boil for 1 min until the sugar dissolves, then add the red onion and simmer for 1 min. Take off the heat, cover, and leave to cool completely.

STEP 2

Mix the broccoli, carrots, cranberries, and cashews in a large bowl. Add the cooled pickled onion, reserving the pickling liquid.

STEP 3

Whisk together the pickling liquid, oil, maple syrup, lemon zest, and juice, along with 2 tbsp cold water. Pour over the vegetables and mix until well coated.

VEGAN ROAST SPICED SQUASH SALAD WITH TAHINI DRESSING

Prep:10 mins

Cook:40 mins

Ingredients

- 320g diced butternut squash
- 3 red onions (320g), cut into wedges
- 2 tbsp rapeseed oil
- 2 tsp smoked paprika
- 1 tsp cumin seeds
- 2 tbsp chopped thyme
- 125g quinoa
- ½ x 85g bag kale
- 2 tbsp pumpkin seeds
- 2 tbsp tahini
- 2 tbsp apple cider vinegar
- 1 garlic clove, finely grated
- 2 x 400g cans lentils or borlotti beans, very well drained

- 50g pomegranate seeds
- Four generous handfuls of rocket

Method
STEP 1

 Preheat the oven to 200C/180C fan/gas 6. Put the squash and onions on a large baking sheet and toss them with 1 tsp of the oil. Spread the paprika, cumin, and thyme out, and then roast for 30 minutes.

STEP 2

Cook the quinoa according to the directions on the package, then drain it well.

STEP 3

Add the kale to the vegetables on the tray, sprinkle the seeds on top, and put the tray back in the oven for 10 minutes.

STEP 4

For the dressing, mix the remaining oil, vinegar, garlic, and 2 tbsp of water with the tahini.

STEP 5

Put the lentils or beans in a bowl and mix in the quinoa. If you're following the Healthy Diet Plan, put half of it in a salad bowl and the rest in two lunchboxes or bowls. Put the vegetables on top, drizzle with the dressing, sprinkle with the pomegranate seeds, and finish with the rocket. Put the other two servings in the fridge for the next day. It will stay cool for up to 3 days.

EGG NIÇOISE SALAD

Prep:10 mins

Cook:10 mins

Ingredients
For the dressing

- 2 tbsp rapeseed oil
- juice one lemon
- 1 tsp balsamic vinegar
- One garlic clove, grated
- ⅓ small pack of basil leaves chopped
- 3 pitted black Kalamata olive, rinsed and chopped

For the salad

- Two eggs
- 250g new potatoes, thickly sliced
- 200g fine green beans
- ½ red onion, very finely chopped
- 14 cherry tomatoes, halved
- Six romaine lettuces leave, torn into bite-sized pieces
- 6 pitted black Kalamata olive, rinsed and halved

Method
STEP 1

Mix the dressing ingredients with 1 tbsp of water in a small bowl.

STEP 2

In the meantime, boil the potatoes for 7 minutes, then add the beans and cook for another 5 minutes, or until the potatoes and beans are just tender. Drain. Boil two eggs for 8 minutes, then peel and cut them in half.

STEP 3

Mix all the salad's other ingredients, except the eggs, with half of the dressing in a large bowl. Place the eggs on top, and then drizzle the rest of the sauce on top.

EGG & PUY LENTIL SALAD WITH TAMARI & WATERCRESS

Prep:10 mins

Cook:35 mins

Ingredients

- 75g dried puy lentils
- 175g cauliflower florets, broken into smaller pieces
- 1 tbsp rapeseed oil, +a drizzle
- One large carrot, chopped into small pieces
- Two celery sticks, chopped into small pieces
- Two garlic cloves
- Three omega-3 enriched eggs
- 1 tbsp wheat-free tamari
- Ten cherry tomatoes halved
- Four spring onions, finely sliced
- Two generous handfuls of watercress, large stems removed

Method
STEP 1

Do this the night before or up to 8 hours before eating if you want to activate the lentils (see tip below). Pour water on them and let them sit at room temperature for a while. Rinse and drain.

STEP 2

When ready to eat, heat the oven to 220C/200C fan/gas 7. Pour some of the oil over the cauliflower and toss it, then roast it for 20 minutes on a baking sheet lined with parchment paper until it is soft and golden around the edges.

STEP 3

In the meantime, put the carrot and celery in a pan with the drained lentils. Pour enough water to cover the lentils, put on the lid, and let them boil for 20 minutes, or until they are soft. Check on them before they are done cooking to see if they are burning dry. If they are, add a little more water.

STEP 4

While they cook, grate the garlic and put it in a large bowl. If you boil the eggs for 6 minutes, the yolks will be soft. When they're done, throw them into cold water and then shell them.

STEP 5

To make a dressing, mix the tamari, oil, and garlic. Check the lentils and drain them if you need to. Add the lentils, tomatoes, spring onions, and watercress to the bowl with the dressing. Place on plates, top with eggs, and drizzle with any sauce left in the bowl.

CHICKEN SATAY SALAD

Prep:15 mins

Cook:5 mins - 10 mins

Ingredients

- 1 tbsp tamari
- 1 tsp medium curry powder
- ¼ tsp ground cumin
- One garlic clove, finely grated
- 1 tsp clear honey
- Two skinless chicken breast fillets (or use turkey breast)
- 1 tbsp crunchy peanut butter (choose a sugar-free version with no palm oil, if possible)
- 1 tbsp sweet chili sauce
- 1 tbsp lime juice
- sunflower oil, for wiping the pan
- 2 Little Gem lettuce hearts, cut into wedges
- ¼ cucumber, halved and sliced
- One banana shallot, halved and thinly sliced
- coriander, chopped
- seeds from ½ pomegranate

Method
STEP 1

Pour the tamari into a large bowl and mix in the curry powder, cumin, garlic, and honey. Blend well. Cut the chicken breasts in half across the middle to make four fillets. Add the fillets to the marinade and mix well to coat. Let the flavors soak into the chicken by putting it in the fridge for at least an hour or overnight.

STEP 2

In the meantime, make a sauce out of the peanut butter, chili sauce, lime juice, and 1 tbsp of water. When you're ready to cook the chicken, use a little oil to wipe down a large nonstick frying pan. Add the chicken, cover, and cook over medium heat for 5–6 minutes, flipping the fillets during the last minute until the chicken is cooked but still moist. Cover and set aside for a few minutes.

STEP 3

While the chicken is resting, toss the lettuce wedges with the cucumber, shallot, coriander, and pomegranate, and then pile them on plates. Put a little sauce on top. Slice the chicken and put it on top of the salad. Then, pour the rest of the sauce on top. Eat the chicken while it's still hot.

SPRING VEGETABLE & CAULIFLOWER TABBOULEH

Prep:15 mins

Cook:15 mins

Ingredients

- One whole cauliflower (about 500g when trimmed)
- 2 tbsp olive oil
- 5 tbsp hot vegetable stock
- 125g pack delicate asparagus, stems cut into small pieces, tips left whole
- One courgette, cut into small cubes
- zest two lemons, juice of 1
- 2 tsp golden caster sugar
- 2 tbsp capers, drained and chopped
- 3 tbsp extra virgin olive oil, +extra to serve

- 50g parsley, leaves only
- small pack mint leaves only
- bunch spring onions, shredded

Method
STEP 1

 Grate the cauliflower on the coarse side of a box grater, stopping when you revery the very hard center in a large pan, and heat 1 tbsp of oil. Add the cauliflower and some seasoning, and cook for 3 minutes, stirring often. Splash the stock, stir, and then cover and cook for another 3–4 minutes. Stir the cauliflower once or twice while it's cooking until it's just soft and the stock is gone. Spread the mixture out on a plate and let it cool. Clean the pan.

STEP 2

Heat the rest of the oil in the pan and add the asparagus stems, courgettes, and seasonings. Fry over high heat for about 3 minutes, or until the food turns golden. Add the asparagus tips and cook for another 2 minutes. Set aside to cool.

STEP 3

Mix the lemon zest and juice with the sugar, capers, oil, and spices. Cut the herbs into small pieces and put them in a large bowl with cauliflower, vegetables, and spring onions. When it's time to eat, add the dressing and stir it in well. Place in a pile on a serving plate, drizzle with a little more oil, and serve with wedges of the remaining lemon that has been zest.

ROASTED CARROT, SPELT, FENNEL & BLOOD ORANGE SALAD

Prep:35 mins

Cook:25 mins

Ingredients

- 400g spelled
- 1 vegetable stock cube
- 4 tbsp extra virgin olive oil
- 400g baby carrots, scrubbed
- Three blood oranges, 2 zested and one juiced
- 1 tbsp olive oil
- 2 tsp clear honey
- 2 fennel bulbs, thinly sliced
- 4 tbsp red wine vinegar
- 1 small red onion, finely chopped
- large bunch of parsley, chopped
- 70g pack pitted dry black olives or 85g councilor (the very small black ones)
- small pack parsley, chopped

Method
STEP 1

Preheat the oven to 200C/180C fan/gas mix and cook the spell with the stock cube according to the package directions. Don't overcook it, as it should still have a little nutty bite. When the spell is done, drain it well and put it on a platter with 1 tbsp of the extra virgin olive oil to keep it from sticking together too much.

STEP 2

In the meantime, put the carrots, olive oil, blood orange zest, and seasonings in a roasting pan and roast for 15 minutes. Carefully mix the fennel with half of the honey. Roast for another 10 minutes, then let it cool for 5 minutes. Remove the pith and peel from the two oranges that have been zested, and then roughly chop or slice them.

STEP 3

Whisk together the blood orange juice, the remaining extra virgin olive oil, 1 tsp honey, red wine vinegar, and some seasonings. Put the orange chunks, red onion, herbs, and olives on top of the spelled, along with the roasted carrots and fennel and any cooking juices. Pour over the dressing, and then mix everything well. The salad will be fine at room temperature for a few hours, but the spelled will soak up the sauce. If you want to make it ahead of time, add half of the dressing when putting it together and stir in the rest just before serving. If you wish, you can mix in the parsley as you do.

CHICKEN, BROCCOLI & BEETROOT SALAD WITH AVOCADO PESTO

Prep:15 mins

Cook:15 mins

Ingredients

- 250g thin-stemmed broccoli
- 2 tsp avocado oil
- 3 skinless chicken breasts
- One red onion, thinly sliced
- 100g bag watercress

- Two raw beetroots (about 175g), peeled and julienned or grated
- 1 tsp nigella seeds

For the avocado pesto

- small pack basil
- One avocado
- ½ garlic cloves, crushed
- 25g walnut halves, crumbled
- 1 tbsp avocado oil
- juice and zest 1 lemon

Method
STEP 1

Bring a large pot of water to a boil, add the broccoli, and cook for 2 minutes. Drain and rinse with cold water. Heat a griddle pan, toss the broccoli in 12 tsp of the rapeseed oil, and cook for 2-3 minutes, turning the broccoli, until it gets a little charred. Set aside to cool. Season the chicken and brush it with the rest of the oil. Grill for 3 to 4 minutes on every side or until done. Let it cool, then cut or shred it into big chunks.

STEP 2

Make the pesto next. Pick some basil leaves and set them aside to put on top of the salad. Put the rest in the food processor's small bowl. Put the avocado flesh, garlic, walnuts, oil, 1 tbsp of lemon juice, 2 to 3 tbsp of cold water, and some seasonings in a food processor. Blend until smooth, then put in a small dish to serve. Pour the rest of the lemon juice over the onions and let them sit for a few minutes.

STEP 3

Put the watercress in a big pile on a big platter. Mix in the broccoli, onion, and lemon juice that they had been sitting in. Beets and chicken go on top, but don't mix them. Sprinkle the reserved basil leaves, lemon zest, and nigella seeds on top, and then serve with the avocado pesto.

AVOCADO PANZANELLA

Prep:20 mins

Serves 4

Ingredients

- 800g mix of ripe tomatoes
- One garlic clove, crushed
- 1½ tbsp capers drained and rinsed
- One ripe avocado, stoned, peeled, and chopped
- One small red onion, very thinly sliced
- 175g ciabatta or crusty loaf
- 4 tbsp extra virgin olive oil
- 2 tbsp red wine vinegar
- a small handful of basil leaves

Method
STEP 1

Cut the tomatoes in half or roughly chop them, depending on how big they are, and put them in a bowl. Season it well, then mix in the garlic, capers, avocado, and onion. Set aside for 10 mins.

STEP 2

In the meantime, break the ciabatta into 3cm pieces and put them in a large bowl or platter. Sprinkle with half of the olive oil, half of the vinegar, and some spices. When ready to serve, pour the tomatoes and their juices over the top. Add the basil leaves and drizzle the rest of the oil and vinegar on top. Give it one last stir, and then serve it right away.

BARBECUED SQUID SALAD

Prep:20 mins

Cook:5 mins

Ingredients
For the squid

- 800g freshly prepared squid
- zest three limes
- 2 tbsp extra virgin olive oil
- Three garlic cloves smashed flat
- 1 ½ tsp mixed peppercorn, crushed

For the salad

- One large red onion, finely sliced
- One large mango, cut into small chunks
- One large red chili, finely shredded (deseeded if you don't like it too hot)
- 400g can black bean, well rinsed then patted dry
- Three ripe avocados
- small pack coriander leaves only, torn
- extra virgin olive oil for drizzling

Method

STEP 1

Heat the grill. In the meantime, put the squid in a marinade for at least 30 minutes and up to 4 hours. First, cut the squid tubes at 5mm-1cm intervals on every side, cutting through most of the flesh but leaving the whole side. If any tubes are big, cut them in half across the width. Put in a bowl that isn't made of metal with the other squid ingredients and let it sit.

STEP 2

For the salad, mix the onion, mango, and chili with the lime juice from the limes you used for the squid and a pinch of salt. Leave for at least 10 minutes or until the onion turns pink. On one side of the bowl, put the beans.

STEP 3

Cut the avocado half, remove the pit, and scoop the flesh into the salad bowl. Add lots of seasonings and sea salt to the squid.

STEP 4

When the grill is ready, cook the squid tubes and tentacles for no more than 1 1/2 minutes. The flesh should change from gray to clear and shrink into a spiral shape where you cut it. Mix the salad ingredients very roughly, pile them on a platter, and top with the hot squid and coriander. Drizzle with extra virgin olive oil and serve with lime wedges.

SESAME CHICKEN SALAD

Prep:10 mins

Cook:10 mins

Ingredients

- Two skinless chicken breasts
- 85g frozen soya bean
- One large carrot, finely cut into thin matchsticks
- Four spring onions, finely sliced
- 140g cherry tomato, halved
- small bunch of coriander, chopped
- small handful Thai
- 85g herb or baby salad leaves
- 1 tsp toasted sesame seeds

For the dressing

- grated zest and juice one small lime
- 1 tsp fish sauce
- 1 tsp sesame oil
- 2 tsp sweet chili sauce

Method
STEP 1

Cover the chicken with cold water and put it in a pan. Pour the soybeans into a steamer. Bring the pan to a slow boil, then cook the chicken and beans together for 8 minutes.

STEP 2

Mix the ingredients for the dressing in a large bowl. When the chicken is done, cut it up and toss it with the beans, carrot, onions, tomatoes, coriander, and basil in the dressing. Mix everything together really well, pile it on the salad leaves, and sprinkle the sesame seeds on top.

LEMONY TUNA & ASPARAGUS SALAD BOX

Prep:5 mins

Cook:8 mins

Ingredients

- Two large eggs
- 200g asparagus, woody ends snapped off, spears halved
- 160g can tuna in spring water
- 1 small red onion, very finely chopped
- 125g cannellini bean from a can, drained
- zest and juice ½ lemon
- 1 tbsp fresh chopped dill
- 1 tsp extra virgin olive oil

Method
STEP 1

Put a steamer over a pan of boiling water. When the water starts to boil, put the eggs in the water and steam the asparagus for 8 minutes.

STEP 2

In the meantime, mix the rest of the ingredients gently and put them on plates or in containers with straight sides. Put the eggs in cold water for a few seconds to cool them down, then peel and cut them into quarters. To the tuna salad, add the eggs and asparagus. It will last for two days in the fridge.

ASPARAGUS SALAD WITH A RUNNY POACHED EGG

Prep:5 mins

Cook:8 mins

Ingredients

- 1 tbsp extra virgin olive oil
- 1 tbsp balsamic vinegar
- 200g peeled cooked beetroot, cut into bite-sized pieces
- Two handfuls of mixed leaves
- ¼ cucumber, cut into batons
- Eight asparagus spears, trimmed
- Two large eggs

Method
STEP 1

Mix the olive oil and vinegar well in a small bowl, then add the beetroot. On two plates, divide the mixed leaves and cucumber.

STEP 2

Cook the asparagus for 2 minutes in a pan of simmering water, then take it out and set it aside. Crack the eggs into the pan and simmer them for 3 minutes until the whites are done, and the yolks start to set but are still runny. Take it out with a slotted spoon and let dry on paper towels.

STEP 3

In the meantime, put the beets on the salad plates, pour the dressing over them, and give them a light toss. To serve, put asparagus and a poached egg on every plate.

CHICKEN GARDEN SALAD WITH ELDERFLOWER DRESSING

Prep:25 mins

Cook:5 mins

Ingredients

- bunch of asparagus (about eight spears), woody ends removed and discarded, cut in half lengthways
- 200g pack sugar snap pea
- 140g fresh or frozen pea
- 1 small cooked chicken, skin and bones tossed, meat shredded
- 250g radish sliced
- One red onion halved and thinly sliced
- One sizeable curly round lettuce or 2 Little Gems, torn
- handful pea shoots

For the elderflower dressing

- 2 tbsp elderflower cordial
- 2 tbsp white wine vinegar
- zest and juice one large lemon
- 3 tbsp extra virgin rapeseed oil

Method
STEP 1

Bring a medium pot to a boil and pour ice-cold water into a large bowl. The asparagus should go into the pan. Add the sugar snaps after 1 minute. After 30 more seconds, add the peas. Cook for 30 seconds more, drain the vegetables and drop them into the icy water. This will cool them quickly and help them keep their crisp texture and bright color. After 1 to 2 minutes, drain the pasta and set it aside in a colander while you get the other ingredients ready.

STEP 2

Dry your bowl, pour in the ingredients for the dressing, add a lot of seasoning, and mix with a whisk. Add the chicken, radishes, onion, cooled and drained vegetables, and lettuce, and gently toss everything together until everything is well coated in the dressing. The easiest way to do this is to use your hands. Put the salad on a big plate and sprinkle the pea shoots on top if you're using them. Serve immediately.

WARM LEMONY COURGETTE SALAD

Prep:10 mins

Cook:5 mins

Ingredients

- Two courgettes
- 1tbsp olive oil
- One lemon, zested, +a squeeze of juice
- One garlic clove, crushed
- ¼ small pack of basil, roughly torn

Method
STEP 1

Use a vegetable peeler to cut the courgettes into wide strips. Throw away the seedy part in the middle. In a large pan, heat the oil over medium heat. Add the lemon zest and garlic and cook for 1 minute. Add the strips of courgette and cook, often stirring, for another 1 to 2 minutes, until the courgettes are just a little bit soft. Mix in the basil and a squeeze of lemon juice.

CARROT, ORANGE & AVOCADO SALAD

Prep:10 mins

Serves 4

Ingredients

- Two oranges, +zest, and juice of 1
- Three carrots were halved lengthways and sliced with a peeler
- 70g bag rocket
- Two avocados, stoned, peeled, and sliced
- 1 tbsp olive oil

Method
STEP 1

Put the carrots, rockets, and avocados in a bowl. Cut the segments out of two of the oranges and put them in the bowl as well. Mix the orange juice, orange zest, and oil with a whisk. Toss the salad and add seasoning.

SRIRACHA & LIME POTATO SALAD

Prep:10 mins

Cook:15 mins

Ingredients

- 750g new potatoes, halved if large
- 80g mayonnaise
- 50g soured cream
- 2 tbsp sriracha

- One lime, zested and juiced
- 1 tsp honey
- Six spring onions, finely sliced
- ½ small bunch of coriander, finely chopped
- ½ tsp chili flakes

Method
STEP 1

Put the potatoes in a large pan of cold, salted water. Bring to a boil, then turn down the heat and simmer for 15–18 minutes, or until the vegetables are soft. Drain and let cool all the way.

STEP 2

Mix the sour cream, Sriracha, lime zest and juice, honey, half of the spring onions, most of the coriander, and some seasoning into the mayonnaise.

STEP 3

Mix the sriracha and mayonnaise and toss it with the cooled potatoes until all of the potatoes are covered. Pour the mixture into a serving bowl and top with the rest of the spring onions, coriander, and chili flakes, if you like.

MISO BROWN RICE & BROCCOLI SALAD WITH FIERY PRAWNS

Prep:15 mins

Cook:25 mins

Ingredients

- 100g brown basmati rice
- 140g ready-shelled frozen edamame beans
- 140g broccoli (about ½ a head), broken into florets

- 1 tbsp white or brown miso paste
- ½ tsp finely grated fresh ginger
- 1 tbsp rice vinegar
- ½ tbsp clear honey
- 2 tsp sesame oil
- 2 tsp vegetable oil
- Three garlic cloves, thinly sliced
- One red chili, thinly sliced
- 200g raw shelled prawn
- Two spring onions, finely sliced
- large pack coriander, roughly chopped

Method
STEP 1

Cook the rice according to the directions on the package. Add the edamame beans during the last three minutes of cooking. Drain well.

STEP 2

In the meantime, steam the broccoli for 4-5 minutes, or until it is soft. Run under icy water, then drain well and dry with a towel. Mix the miso, ginger, vinegar, honey, sesame oil, and spices in a small bowl.

STEP 3

In a pan that doesn't stick, heats the vegetable oil. Add the garlic and half of the chili and cook slowly for a few minutes, careful not to let it burn. Add the shrimp, a lot of black pepper, and a little bit of salt. Turn up the heat and let the prawns cook for a few minutes until they are done. Mix the cooked rice, spring onions, coriander, and broccoli with the miso dressing. Season and mix well. Place the spicy prawns on top, sprinkle the rest of the chili on top, and serve.

MUSTARDY BEETROOT & LENTIL SALAD

- Prep:5 mins
- Cook:20 mins

Ingredients

- 200g puy lentils
- 1 tbsp wholegrain mustard
- 1 ½ tbsp extra virgin olive oil
- 300g pack cooked beetroot, sliced
- large handful of tarragon, roughly chopped

Method
STEP 1

If you aren't using lentils that are already cooked, cook the lentils according to the directions on the package, drain them, and let them cool. Mix the mustard, oil, and seasonings to make a dressing.

STEP 2

Pour the dressing over the lentils in a bowl and mix well. Mix in the beets, tarragon, and a bit of seasoning, then serve.

LATE-SUMMER TOMATO & CARROT SALAD

Prep:15 mins

Serves 6

Ingredients

- 600g mixed ripe tomatoes, such as red and yellow cherry, plum, and medium vine
- Two medium carrots, peeled and finely shredded or grated
- bunch spring onions, trimmed and finely chopped
- One red chili, deseeded and finely chopped
- 25g pumpkin seed
- 3 tbsp extra virgin olive oil
- 2 tbsp balsamic vinegar

Method
STEP 1

Chop the big tomatoes and cut the cherry tomatoes in half, then put them all in a big serving bowl. Mix the carrots, spring onions, chili, and pumpkin seeds.

STEP 2

Mix the balsamic vinegar, the extra virgin olive oil, a pinch of salt, and a good grinding of black pepper. Pour over the tomatoes and mix.

SWEETCORN SALSA

Prep:15 mins

Cook:5 mins

Ingredients

- Four fresh corn cobs
- 2 vine tomatoes, chopped
- ½ red onion, chopped
- 1 red pepper, deseeded and chopped
- One avocado, stoned, peeled, and chopped
- One jalapeño pepper, deseeded and finely chopped
- a handful of coriander, roughly chopped
- juice three limes
- 75g feta cheese

Method
STEP 1

Boil the corn until it's soft, about 5 minutes. Run the machine under cold water and let it drain well. Cut the corn kernels off the cob and put them in a big bowl.

STEP 2

Mix well after adding the tomatoes, onion, red pepper, avocado, jalapeno pepper, coriander, lime juice, and spices. Crumble the feta on top before serving.

RUNNER BEAN, SMOKED TROUT & POTATO SALAD

Prep:15 mins

Cook:15 mins

Ingredients

- 500g new potato, scrubbed and cut in half
- 300g runner bean, trimmed and sliced
- Four spring onions, sliced
- ½ bunch parsley, roughly chopped
- 150g pack smoked trout, flaked

For the dressing

- 50ml extra-virgin olive oil
- juice ½ lemon
- 2 tbsp red wine vinegar
- 2 tsp wholegrain mustard
- 1 tbsp horseradish sauce

Method
STEP 1

Put all the ingredients for the dressing in a jar and shake it well. Cook the potatoes in salted water that is boiling for 10 minutes, or until they are just tender. Drain. Cook the beans in salted water that is burning for 10 minutes, or until they are soft. Then, put them in a bowl of ice water and drain.

STEP 2

Mix the warm potatoes, beans, half of the spring onions, half of the parsley, and half of the dressing. Spread on a plate, then sprinkle smoked trout on top. Spread the rest of the spring onions on top, drizzle the rest of the dressing on top, and serve or let everyone help themselves.

LENTIL SALAD WITH TAHINI DRESSING

Prep:15 mins

Cook:20 mins

Ingredients

- 2 tbsp cold-pressed rapeseed oil
- 320g sweet potatoes, cut into cubes
- Two large carrots, cut into thin sticks (320g)
- Two large courgettes (375g) cut into chunks
- Two medium red onions, halved and sliced
- 1 tsp cumin seeds
- 2 tbsp finely chopped ginger
- 2 tbsp pumpkin seeds
- 2 x 390g cans green lentils, drained
- 2 tsp vegetable bouillon powder
- One lemon, zested
- a good handful of mint, roughly chopped
- a handful of parsley, roughly chopped
- 2.5-3 tbsp tahini
- One garlic clove, finely grated
- 2 x 120g pot bio yogurt
- a little smoked paprika to serve

Method
STEP 1

Heat the oil in a big wok that doesn't stick. Add the sweet potato and cook for 5 minutes, often stirring, until it softens. Put a lid on the pan if it starts to brown too quickly. Add the carrot, courgette, onion, cumin, and ginger, then cook over high heat, stirring often, until the vegetables are soft and a little charred. Near the end, stir in the seeds so they can cook for a few minutes. Take the pot off the heat and add the lentils, bouillon powder, lemon zest, mint, and parsley.

STEP 2

Mix the tahini, garlic, yogurt, and 1 tbsp of water to make a dressing. Put the lentil salad in bowls and top with the sauce and paprika if you're using it. If you're following our Healthy Diet Plan, put two servings in containers and put them in the fridge until you're ready to eat them.

ALLOTMENT SALAD

Prep:20 mins

Cook:10 mins

Ingredients

- Eight asparagus spears halved
- 250g green beans, halved
- 250g long-stem broccoli, chopped into 2cm lengths
- 200g peas, fresh or frozen
- Eight radishes, sliced
- One pointed cabbage, shredded
- Four spring onions, sliced
- a handful of mint leaves, chopped

For the dressing

- 4 tbsp olive oil
- 1 tbsp Dijon mustard
- One lemon, juiced

Method
STEP 1

Mix all of the ingredients for the dressing in a bowl and season it well.

STEP 2

Bring a pot of salted water to a boil and pour ice water into a bowl. Cook the asparagus for 2 minutes, then use a slotted spoon to move it to the iced water. Beans: Cook for 4 minutes, then repeat. Broccoli: Cook for 212 minutes, then peas (cook for 1 min). Drain and use kitchen paper to dry.

STEP 3

Mix with the radishes, cabbage, spring onions, and mint in a bowl. The dressing should be served on the side.

TUNA, ASPARAGUS & WHITE BEAN SALAD

Prep:10 mins

Cook:5 mins

Ingredients
- One large bunch of asparagus
- 2 x cans tuna steaks in water, drained
- 2 x cans cannellini beans in water, drained
- One red onion, very finely chopped
- 2 tbsp capers
- 1 tbsp olive oil
- 1 tbsp red wine vinegar
- 2 tbsp tarragon, finely chopped

Method
STEP 1

Cook the asparagus for 4-5 minutes in a large pot of boiling water until it is soft. Drain well, let cool under running water, and then cut into pieces about the size of your finger. In a large serving bowl, mix the tuna, beans, onion, capers, and asparagus.

STEP 2

Pour the mixture of oil, vinegar, and tarragon over the salad. Cool until you're ready to serve.

PULLED CHICKEN SALAD

Prep:20 mins

Serves 5

Ingredients

- One small roasted chicken, about 1kg
- ½ red cabbage, cored and finely sliced
- Three carrots, coarsely grated or finely shredded
- Five spring onions, finely sliced on the diagonal
- Two red chilies, halved and thinly sliced
- small bunch of coriander, roughly chopped, including stalks
- Two heaped tbsp roasted salted peanuts, roughly crushed

For the dressing

- 3 ½ tbsp hoisin sauce
- 1 ½ tbsp toasted sesame oil

Method
STEP 1

Mix the ingredients for the dressing in a small bowl and put it aside.

STEP 2

Take the meat off the chicken, shred it into big pieces, and put it in a big bowl. Add the cabbage, carrots, spring onions, chilies, and half of the coriander. Mix with the dressing, pile on a serving plate, and then sprinkle the rest of the coriander and peanuts on top.

LENTIL & TOMATO SALAD

Prep:5 mins

Cook:20 mins

Ingredients

- 250g dried Puy or green lentil, rinsed
- juice ½ lime and juice ½ lemon
- 1 tbsp white wine or cider vinegar
- One red onion, thinly sliced into rings
- 2 tbsp extra-virgin olive oil
- 1 tsp ground cumin
- One small garlic clove, crushed
- 2 tbsp mango chutney
- a handful of coriander, roughly chopped
- 250g cherry vine tomato, halved
- 85g baby spinach, washed and thoroughly dried

Method
STEP 1

Boil the lentils as directed on the package, then drain, rinse well, and drain well again.

STEP 2

In the meantime, mix the citrus juices, vinegar, and a pinch of salt in a salad bowl. Toss in the onion rings, which will soften and turn pink after a few minutes. Mix the oil, cumin, garlic, and chutney, then add it to the onions along with the lentils, coriander, tomatoes, spinach, and a lot of spices.

MOROCCAN AUBERGINE & CHICKPEA SALAD

Prep:15 mins

Cook:20 mins

Ingredients

- Two aubergines
- 2-3 tbsp olive oil
- 400g can chickpeas
- good bunch of fresh coriander, roughly chopped
- One red onion, finely chopped

For the dressing

- 1 tsp every paprika and ground cumin
- 1 tsp clear honey
- One lemon, juice only
- 4 tbsp olive oil

Method
STEP 1

Cut the aubergines into thin slices and put them on a grill rack. Brush the meat with a bit of oil, sprinkle it with salt and pepper, and grill until it turns brown. Turn them over, brush them with oil, and season them again. Cook for another 8 to 10 minutes, or until they are soft. Take the slices off the grill and cut everyone into four pieces.

STEP 2

Drain and rinse the chickpeas, then add eggplant, coriander, and red onion to a bowl. Mix the ingredients for the dressing in a jar with a screw-on lid, shake it well, and then use it to dress the salad.

HERBY QUINOA, FETA & POMEGRANATE SALAD

Prep:10 mins

Cook:15 mins

Ingredients

- 300g quinoa
- One red onion, finely chopped
- 85g raisins or sultana
- 100g feta cheese, crumbled
- 200g pomegranate seeds from tub or fruit
- 85g toasted pine nuts or toasted flaked almonds
- a small pack of every coriander, flat leaf parsley, and mint, roughly chopped
- juice three lemon
- 1 tsp sugar

Method
STEP 1

Cook the quinoa according to the directions on the package. It should be soft but still have some bite to it. Drain well and spread out on a platter or a wide, shallow bowl to cool quickly and steam dry.

STEP 2

When the quinoa is almost incredible, mix it with the rest of the ingredients and a lot of seasoning.

WARM CAULIFLOWER SALAD

Prep:15 mins

Cook:35 mins

Ingredients

- One cauliflower, broken into florets
- 2 tbsp olive oil
- One red onion, thinly sliced
- 3 tbsp sherry vinegar
- 1½ tbsp honey
- 3 tbsp raisins
- small bunch of dill snipped
- 3 tbsp toasted, flaked almond
- 50g baby spinach

Method
STEP 1

Preheat oven to 200C/180C fan/gas 6. Toss the cauliflower with olive oil, season it, and roast it for 15 minutes. Stir in the red onion, and roast for another 15–20 minutes, until the onion is soft.

STEP 2

While the cauliflower is roasting, mix the vinegar, honey, raisins, and seasonings.

STEP 3

When the cauliflower is done, mix the dressing, dill, almonds, and spinach.

TUNA RICE SALAD

Prep:30 mins

Serves 8

Ingredients

- approx 900g/2lb cold cooked rice (about 400g/140uncesuncooked rice)
- 400g tuna in springwater
- 200g frozen petit pois, defrosted
- Two red peppers, peeled with a potato peeler, deseeded and diced
- Three tomatoes, chopped into small chunks
- Five spring onions, finely sliced
- bunch flat-leaf parsley, chopped
- large handful of stoned green olives, roughly chopped
- 4 tbsp mayonnaise
- juice 1 lemon
- 2 tbsp extra-virgin olive oil

Method
STEP 1

If the cooked rice is stuck together, break it up in a large mixing bowl. Flake in the tuna, and then mix in the peas, peppers, tomatoes, spring onions, parsley, and olives, if you're using them.

STEP 2

Mix the mayonnaise, lemon juice, and olive oil. Add salt and pepper to taste. Cover the bowl with cling film or put it in a large plastic container, and let your family serve themselves whenever they are hungry.

PASTA SALAD WITH TUNA MAYO

Prep:20 mins

Cook:20 mins

Ingredients

- 250g wholemeal penne
- 240g bio yogurt
- 2 tsp English mustard powder
- 2 tbsp extra virgin olive oil
- 4tsp apple cider vinegar
- One red onion, finely chopped
- a handful of basil leaves, finely chopped
- 320g tuna in spring water
- Two red peppers, deseeded and diced
- 340g can sweetcorn, drained

Method

STEP 1

Boil the pasta for 10 minutes, until it is al dente, then drain and rinse under cold running water. Drain again. In the meantime, stir together the yogurt, mustard, olive oil, vinegar, onion, and basil in a large bowl. Add the tuna, red peppers, and sweetcorn and stir again.

STEP 2

Mix the sauce into the pasta, then serve in bowls or put it in containers to take to work or on a picnic. Will keep in the fridge, covered, until the next day.

BUTTER BEAN & TOMATO SALAD

Total time20 mins

Ready in 15-20 minutes

Ingredients

- 420g can butter beans, drained and rinsed
- 500g cherry tomato, quartered
- 2small green or yellow courgettes (about 300g/10Ouncesin total), chopped into small dice
- One small red onion, chopped
- 15-20g pack fresh coriander, chopped
- 2 tbsp lemon juice
- 3 tbsp olive oil
- 1 tsp ground cumin

Method
STEP 1

Put all the ingredients in a bowl and mix well with salt and pepper. Cover and let sit at room temperature until ready to serve. This salad can be made and chilled the day before.

STEP 2

On serving day, let the salad come to room temperature and give it a good stir.

PUY LENTIL, SPICED ROAST CARROT & FETA SALAD

Prep:10 mins

Cook:30 mins

Ingredients

- 2 tbsp olive oil
- 1 tbsp cumin seeds
- 500g carrots, peeled, halved, and cut into batons
- 1 tbsp clear honey
- 250g pouch cooked Puy lentils
- One red onion, finely sliced
- ½ lemon, juiced
- large handful of mint leaves, roughly chopped
- 100g lamb's lettuce
- 85g feta cheese, crumbled

Method
STEP 1

Preheat the oven to 200C/180C fan/gas 6. Mix half of the oil, the cumin, the carrots, and spices in a shallow roasting pan. Roast for 25 minutes, turning the meat over halfway through. Pour the honey on top, stir, and roast for five more minutes.

STEP 2

In the meantime, heat the lentils with the onion, lemon juice, the rest of the oil, salt, and pepper over low heat. Let it cool down a bit while you finish cooking the carrots.

STEP 3

Mix the lentils dressed with the mint and lamb's lettuce. Place warm carrots with spices on top, and then sprinkle with feta.

CHICKEN TACO SALAD

Prep:10 mins

Serves 1

Ingredients

- ¼ tsp olive oil
- 2 tbsp low-fat soured cream
- 1 tsp white wine vinegar
- 1 Baby Gem lettuce, shredded
- 50g sweetcorn, drained
- Five cherry tomatoes halved
- 75g cooked BBQ chicken
- juice one lime
- ½ small avocado, peeled and chopped
- One corn taco shell, broken into pieces

Method
STEP 1

Mix the oil, sour cream, and vinegar to make the dressing. Put in the refrigerator.

STEP 2

Put the chicken, lettuce, sweet corn, and tomatoes in a lunchbox. Mix the lime juice into the avocado, then put it on top. Bring the sauce to the side.

STEP 3

To serve, put the tacos all over the salad.

ROASTED VEG & COUSCOUS SALAD

Prep:10 mins

Cook:40 mins

Ingredients

- One red and one yellow pepper halved and deseeded
- ½ butternut squash
- Two courgettes, thickly sliced
- 4 garlic cloves, leave the skin on
- 3 tbsp extra-virgin olive oil
- One red onion, thickly sliced
- 1 tsp cumin seeds
- 1 tbsp harissa paste
- 50g whole blanched almonds
- 250g couscous
- 300ml hot vegetable stock
- zest and juice one lemon
- 20g pack mint, roughly chopped

Method
STEP 1

 Preheat oven to 200C/180C fan/gas 6. Cut the peppers and squash into pieces that are easy to eat (leave the skin on the squash). Put all of the vegetables on a baking sheet, add the garlic, 2 tbsp of oil, and seasonings, and mix. Roast for 20 minutes. Onion, cumin, harissa, and almonds should be added. Roast for 20 more minutes, then let it cool.

STEP 2

Pour the stock over the couscous, cover, and let it sit for 10 minutes. Use a fork to fluff up.

STEP 3

Mix the zest, juice, and the rest of the oil in a bowl. Squeeze the garlic pulp out of the skins and into the bowl. Mash it up well, and then mix in the mint. Pour over the vegetables, and then mix in the couscous.

MINTY GRIDDLED CHICKEN & EVERY SALAD

Prep:10 mins

Cook:15 mins

Ingredients

- One lime, zested and juiced
- 1 tbsp rapeseed oil
- 2 tbsp mint, finely chopped, and +a few leaves to serve
- One garlic clove, finely grated
- Two skinless chicken breast fillets (300g)
- 160g fine beans, trimmed and halved
- Two peaches (200g), every cut into eight thick wedges
- One red onion, cut into wedges
- One large Little Gem lettuce (165g), roughly shredded
- ½ x 60g pack rocket
- One small avocado, stoned and sliced

- 240g cooked new potatoes

Method
STEP 1

Mix the lime zest, lime juice, oil, and mint. Put half of the mixture in a bowl with the garlic. Cut the chicken into thin slices at an angle and add them to the garlic mixture. Add a lot of black pepper and toss everything together.

STEP 2

In a pan of water, cook the beans for 3–4 minutes, or until they are tender. In the meantime, cook the chicken and onion on a grill for a few minutes on every side until they are done and soft. Place on a plate, then quickly cook the peaches on a grill. If you don't have a griddle pan, you can use a nonstick frying pan with a drop of oil.

STEP 3

Mix the warm beans and onion with the rest of the mint mixture. Pile the mixture on a platter or into shallow bowls for every person. On top, place the avocado, peaches, and chicken. Then, sprinkle the mint on top. Serve the potatoes while they are still hot.

SPRING CELEBRATION SALAD

Prep:20 mins

Cook:30 mins

Ingredients
- 300g Jersey Royal new potatoes, scrubbed clean but not peeled, big ones cut in half
- One mint sprig

- Two eggs
- 200g asparagus, woody stalks removed and saved
- 50g fresh peas, podded
- 4 tbsp mayonnaise
- One green apple, cored and finely chopped
- Three spring onions, finely sliced
- 1 tsp capers, drained
- 2 tbsp olive oil
- 1 tbsp white wine vinegar
- 1 Little Gem lettuce, leaves washed and dried, heart split in two
- 3-4 handfuls of soft herbs

For the garlic croutons

- Two slices of sourdough or white baguette
- drizzle of olive oil
- Three garlic cloves

Method
STEP 1

Preheat oven to 200C/180C fan/gas 6. Drizzle some olive oil on the bread and season it, then roast it in the oven, turning it over halfway through, for 12 to 15 minutes, or until it is golden and crispy. Once the bread is baked, rub it with the raw garlic and break or cut it into croutons.

STEP 2

Bring some water to a boil in a pan. Add the potatoes, mint, and 1 tsp of salt, and let the mixture simmer for 15 minutes, or until the potatoes are soft. Don't worry about overcooking them; they're much better when they're soft than when they're chalky. Remove the mint sprig and drain the potatoes.

STEP 3

While that happens, bring another pan of water to a boil and put the eggs in it. Bring to a boil again and cook for 6 minutes. Drain the eggs, then run them under cold water to cool them down. Tap the eggs on the table, and then peel them.

STEP 4

Bring to a boil another pan of salted water. Cut every asparagus spear into three pieces and boil them for 3–4 minutes, or until they are tender. Use a slotted spoon to take them out and then rinse them in cold water. Bring the water back to a boil and sprinkle a bit of sugar. Put the peas in the water and cook them until they are soft (about 2-3 mins). Drain.

STEP 5

Mix the potatoes, apple, spring onions, and capers with 2 tbsp of mayonnaise. Mix the olive oil and white wine vinegar, add seasoning, and then drizzle the mixture over the lettuce, soft herbs, asparagus, and peas. Spread the remaining mayonnaise on your plate, add the potatoes and salad, cut the eggs in half, and add more mayonnaise if you want. Add the croutons and extra herbs to the top.

ZINGY SALMON & BROWN RICE SALAD

Prep:15 mins

Cook:25 mins

Ingredients

- 200g brown basmati rice
- 200g frozen soya beans, defrosted
- Two salmon fillets

- One cucumber, diced
- small bunch of spring onions, sliced
- small bunch of coriander, roughly chopped
- zest and juice one lime
- One red chili, diced, deseeded if you like
- 4 tsp light soy sauce

Method
STEP 1

Cook the rice according to the directions on the package. Add the soya beans 3 minutes before the rice is done. Drain it and run cold water over it to cool it down.

STEP 2

In the meantime, put the salmon on a plate and microwave it on High for 3 minutes, or until it is fully cooked. Let it cool, use a fork to peel off the skin, and then flake.

STEP 3

Mix the salmon, cucumber, spring onions, and coriander into the rice and beans gently. Mix the lime zest and juice, chili, and soy sauce in a separate bowl, then pour it over the rice before serving.

STEAK & VIETNAMESE NOODLE SALAD

Prep:15 mins

Cook:10 mins

Ingredients
- 83g brown rice noodles
- 1 tsp rapeseed oil
- 250g fillet steak

- Two carrots, peeled into ribbons
- ½ Chinese cabbage, shredded
- Four spring onions, sliced
- One small pack of coriander, roughly chopped

For the dressing

- One red chili, seeds removed and thinly sliced
- One lime, juiced
- 2 tsp soft brown sugar
- 1 tsp rice wine vinegar
- One garlic clove, finely chopped
- ½ tbsp fish sauce

Method
STEP 1

Mix all dressing ingredients in a bowl with 1 tbsp of water until the sugar is dissolved.

STEP 2

Follow the directions on the package to cook the noodles, then put them in a bowl of cold water to cool down. Drain the noodles, then toss them with the carrot, cabbage, spring onion, and dressing.

STEP 3

In a frying pan, heat the oil over high heat. Season the steak, then cook it to your liking. For medium rare, cook it for 2 to 3 minutes on every side. Let it sit for 5 minutes, and then cut it. To serve, divide the salad and steak slices among bowls and sprinkle coriander on top.

CELERY SALAD

Prep:30 mins

Serves 6

Ingredients

- 200g bulgur wheat
- One bunch celery
- One dessert apple
- juice one lemon
- 4 tbsp olive oil
- a handful of toasted hazelnuts, roughly chopped
- One red chili, deseeded and chopped
- large handful of pomegranate seeds
- small bunch of parsley, chopped
- small bunch of mint, chopped
- small bunch of tarragon, chopped

Method
STEP 1

Pour enough boiling water into a large bowl to cover the bulgur wheat. Cover the bowl with plastic wrap and let it sit for 30 minutes so that all the water can be absorbed.

STEP 2

While that happens, separate the celery sticks and set the leaves aside. Cut the celery into skinny slices and roughly chop the leaves. Cut the apple into thin strips and toss them with some lemon juice. Make a dressing by mixing the remaining lemon juice with the oil and some seasonings in a bowl.

STEP 3

Use a fork to fluff up the bulgur in a gentle way. Mix the chopped apple and celery into the bulgur, then add the nuts, chili, pomegranate seeds, and herbs. Pour over the dressing, and then gently toss everything together. Place the celery leaves on top and serve.

STEAK, BEETROOT, HORSERADISH & WARM LENTIL SALAD

Prep:10 mins

Cook:10 mins

Ingredients

- 1 tbsp hot horseradish sauce
- 2 tbsp Greek yogurt
- ½ tsp honey
- One lemon, juiced
- 200g fillet steak
- 1½ tbsp cold pressed rapeseed oil
- Two garlic cloves
- 200g frozen peas
- 250g pouch pre-cooked puy lentils
- 120g runner beans, sliced
- 200g pre-cooked beetroot, cut into wedges
- ½ small pack of dill, chopped
- two handfuls rocket

Method
STEP 1

Mix the horseradish, yogurt, and honey with a whisk. Add lemon juice as needed and season.

STEP 2

Add a little salt and black pepper to all sides of the steak. Heat 1 tbsp of oil in a pan that doesn't stick. Add the steak and cook it to your taste, about 2 to 3 minutes per side for medium rare. Put somewhere to rest.

STEP 3

Put the pan back on the stove, add the rest of the oil and garlic, and then add the peas, lentils, beans, and beetroot. Stir the mixture for a few minutes until the peas and beetroot are warm. Take it off the heat and add the rest of the lemon juice, dill, and rocket.

STEP 4

Cut the steak into thin slices. On two plates, divide the lentil salad, place the steak in the middle, and drizzle the dressing on top.

GARDEN SALMON SALAD

Prep:15 mins

Serves 4

Ingredients

- Two courgettes
- 100g fresh shelled peas
- Eight radishes halved
- 3 tbsp avocado oil
- One large lemon, zested and juiced
- 2 tbsp natural yogurt
- 75g pea shoots

- Four poached salmon fillets, skin removed and flaked into large chunks
- 2 tbsp mixed seeds
- 1/2 small bunch dill, fronds picked

Method
STEP 1

Peel the courgettes and cut them into long, thin strips. Discard the soft, seeded center. Mix the ribbons of courgette, peas, and radishes in a large bowl. Mix the oil, lemon zest and juice, and yogurt, then toss with the vegetables.

STEP 2

Put the pea shoots, vegetables that have been dressed, and big pieces of salmon on a big platter. Finish with a good grinding of black pepper and a sprinkle of dill and mixed seeds.

VEGGIE HUMMUS PASTA SALAD

Prep:20 mins

Cook:10 mins

Ingredients

- 400g can chickpeas, drained and liquid reserved
- 1 tbsp tahini
- 2 tbsp extra virgin olive oil
- ½ garlic clove
- ½ lemon, zested and juiced
- 250g short pasta of your choice
- 50g baby spinach, roughly chopped
- 200g cherry tomatoes halved

- ¼ cucumber quartered lengthways and cut into small triangles
- 75g pitted olives of your choice, roughly chopped

Method
STEP 1

Get the kettle to boil. Pour half of the chickpeas into a food processor. Add about half of the reserved liquid from the can (the liquid should come up to just below the level of the chickpeas in the blender), the tahini, olive oil, garlic, lemon zest, and juice and some seasoning. Blend until the hummus is smooth and loose. Check the spices.

STEP 2

Follow the directions on the package to cook the pasta. Drain and rinse under cold running water for a few seconds until cool. Save a cup of the cooking water.

STEP 3

Mix the cooked pasta, spinach, tomatoes, cucumbers, olives, the rest of the chickpeas, and the hummus dressing together in a large bowl until everything is well-coated. If the dressing is too thick, add a splash of the pasta water you saved. Covered and kept cold for up to 6 hours, or 2 hours in an airtight container in a cool bag. Before serving, add a splash of water to the dressing to make it easier to spread.

CHICKEN PASTA SALAD

- Prep:10 mins
- Cook:20 mins

Ingredients

- One red pepper, deseeded and thickly sliced
- One red onion, thickly sliced
- 1 tbsp olive oil
- 300g penne or fusilli pasta
- Four skinless chicken breasts
- 2 tbsp every chopped thyme and oregano
- pinch dried chili flakes
- Two garlic cloves, crushed
- 150g pack, cherry tomato, halved
- 50g bag rocket
- 1 tbsp white wine vinegar

Method
STEP 1

Preheat oven to 220C/200C fan/gas 7. Mix the pepper and onion with 1 tsp of oil and roast for 20 minutes.

STEP 2

Follow the directions on the package to cook the pasta. Drain and put away.

STEP 3

In the meantime, put the chicken breasts between two sheets of plastic wrap and use a rolling pin to flatten them until they are about 1 cm thick. Mix the rest of the oil, herbs, chili, and garlic, and then rub it all over the chicken. Heat a griddle or grill and cook for 3–4 minutes on every side.

STEP 4

On a cutting board, slice the chicken and scrape any juices into the pasta. Add the roasted onion and pepper, cherry tomatoes, rocket, vinegar, salt, and pepper. Mix everything and eat it hot or cold.

SUPERHEALTHY SALMON SALAD

Prep:20 mins

Cook:5 mins

Ingredients

- 100g couscous
- 1 tbsp olive oil
- Two salmon fillets
- 200g sprouting broccoli, roughly shredded, more giant stalks removed
- juice one lemon
- seeds from half a pomegranate
- a small handful of pumpkin seeds
- Two handfuls watercress
- olive oil and extra lemon wedges to serve

Method
STEP 1

Bring water to a boil in a tier steamer. Season the couscous, and then mix in 1 tsp of oil. Pour enough boiling water over the couscous to cover it by 1 cm, then set it aside. When the water in the steamer boils, put the broccoli in the water, and then put the salmon on the top tier. Cook for 3 minutes, or until the broccoli is soft and the salmon is done. To cool it down, drain the broccoli and run it under cold water.

STEP 2

Mix the rest of the oil and lemon juice. Mix the lemon dressing, broccoli, pomegranate seeds, and pumpkin seeds into the couscous. Cut the watercress roughly and mix it into the couscous at the last minute. Serve with lemon wedges to squeeze over the salmon and extra olive oil to drizzle, if you like.

MISO BROCCOLI, EGG & QUINOA SALAD

Prep:5 mins

Cook:15 mins

Ingredients

- 100g thin-stemmed broccoli spears
- One medium egg
- 2 tsp white miso paste
- One lime, juiced
- 125g cooked quinoa
- 70g frozen peas, defrosted
- Three radishes, thinly sliced
- ½ tbsp sesame seeds

Method
STEP 1

Bring some water to a boil in a pan. Add the broccoli and cook for 3 minutes. Then, use a slotted spoon to remove the broccoli and set it aside to cool. Put the egg in the water and let it cook slowly for six minutes. Drain and put in a bowl of cold water to cool.

STEP 2

In a small bowl, mix the miso and lime juice. Then, toss the quinoa, peas, radishes, and cooked broccoli with the mixture. Put the salad in your lunchbox or a container that keeps air out. Peel the egg, cut it in half, and place every half on top of the quinoa. Sprinkle the sesame seeds on top.

STORECUPBOARD TUNA BEAN SALAD

Prep:20 mins - 30 mins

Serves 4

Ingredients

- 500g pack salad potato, such as Charlotte
- 4 tbsp olive oil, +extra for drizzling
- 1 tbsp lemon juice
- ½ tsp chili powder
- One plump garlic clove, finely chopped
- 410g can cannellini bean, drained and rinsed
- One small red onion or half a medium one, finely chopped
- a good handful of parsley, chopped
- 200g can tuna, drained
- 110g bag mixed salad leaf and herbs

Method
STEP 1

Boil the potatoes until they are soft, about 15 minutes. In the meantime, make the sauce. In a bowl big enough to hold all the salad, mix the oil, lemon juice, chili powder, and garlic. Add the onion, parsley, and cannellini beans.

STEP 2

When the potatoes are cool enough to handle, drain them and cut them in half along their length. Now, stir the potatoes and tuna into the salad gently. Place on a bed of salad leaves that have a little extra olive oil drizzled on top.

SUMMER SALAD

Prep:20 mins

Serves 6

Ingredients

- Three carrots
- bunch radishes
- Two courgettes
- half a small red onion
- a small handful of mint leaves, roughly torn

For the dressing

- 1 tbsp white wine vinegar
- 1 tsp Dijon mustard
- 1 tbsp mayonnaise
- 2 tbsp olive oil

Method
STEP 1

 Shred the carrots and put them in a big bowl. Cut the radishes and courgettes into thin slices and chop the onion very finely. Mix all the vegetables and the mint leaves in the bowl.

STEP 2

Whisk the vinegar, mustard, and mayonnaise together until the mixture is smooth. Then, whisk in the oil slowly. Salt and pepper to taste, then drizzle over salad and mix well. Leftovers can be kept in the fridge for up to 24 hours in a container with a lid.

SMOKY AUBERGINE & RED PEPPER SALAD

Prep:20 mins

Cook:45 mins

Ingredients

- 30g walnuts
- Two pitta bread, sliced into strips
- 1 tsp za'atar
- 2 tbsp rapeseed oil
- Two medium aubergines
- 4-6 Romano peppers
- a handful of flatleaf parsley, finely chopped
- ½ tbsp extra virgin olive oil
- 1 tbsp sherry vinegar
- 40g feta or vegetarian feta
- a few mints leaves to garnish

Method
STEP 1

Preheat oven to 180C/160C fan/gas 4. Put the pitta strips in one baking dish and the walnuts in another. Sprinkle some za'atar, salt, and pepper on the pita strips, then drizzle them with oil. Put both pans in the oven for 10 minutes, then take out the walnuts. For another 3–5 minutes, roast the pita strips until they are golden and crisp. Take out of the oven.

STEP 2

In the meantime, use a fork to poke holes all over the eggplants and peppers. If you have a gas stove, set the rings to medium-high heat (or better still, light the barbecue and move the coals to one side). Put the eggplants over the heat until they fall apart, then use tongs to flip them and cook the other side. Keep turning until the whole thing is charred and soft through. Do the same thing with the red peppers until they are blackened and soft. If you don't have a gas stove or barbecue, heat your grill to high (about 275C) and put the pricked eggplants and peppers on a baking tray lined with foil and a little oil. 10–15 minutes on every side until charred and soft. Set aside.

STEP 3

Take the eggplants and peppers off the heat and let them cool before putting them on a cutting board. Peel the peppers' skin carefully, cut them in half, and scoop out the seeds. Cut the aubergines in half and use a spoon to scrape the soft flesh into a bowl. Even if some charred skin falls into the bowl, don't worry about it. It will add flavor, but try to keep the pieces small.

STEP 4

Tear the pepper into strips and add them to the aubergine in the bowl. Add almost all of the chopped parsley, season with salt and pepper, and then mix in the olive oil and vinegar. Place on a platter and sprinkle with walnuts and feta. Add some extra parsley and mint leaves to the top.

AUBERGINE & GOAT'S CHEESE SALAD WITH MINT-CHILLI DRESSING

Prep:15 mins

Cook:25 mins

Ingredients

- Two aubergines
- 1 tbsp extra-virgin olive oil
- Two pieces of lavash bread or pitta bread
- 175g cherry plum tomato, halved or quartered
- Four large handfuls of salad leaves
- Two shallots, thinly sliced
- 50g hard goat's cheese

For the mint-chili dressing

- 3 tbsp balsamic vinegar
- 2 tbsp extra-virgin olive oil
- One large handful of mint leaves, finely chopped
- One red chili, seeds removed, finely chopped
- One shallot, finely chopped

Method
STEP 1

Preheat oven to 200C/180C fan/gas 6. Cut the eggplant into 3 cm pieces. Sprinkle with salt and olive oil. Put them on a baking sheet and roast them for 25 minutes or until they are browned.

STEP 2

Put the pieces of bread on a baking sheet. Before the eggplant is done, put the bread in the oven and bake it for 8 minutes.

STEP 3

To make the mint-chili dressing, put all of the ingredients in a small bowl and mix them. About a third of the sauce should be combined with the aubergine. The rest of the dressing should be poured over the salad. Put the tomatoes, salad leaves, shallots, dressed eggplant, and crisp bread on a large platter. Pour the dressing you saved on top and sprinkle the goat cheese on top.

BUTTERNUT, CHICKPEA, FETA & PICKLED RADISH SALAD

Prep:15 mins

Cook:50 mins

Ingredients

- 2 tbsp olive oil
- 1 tbsp rose harissa
- One butternut squash, skin on, seeds removed, and cut into large wedges
- 2 x 400g can chickpeas, drained
- 2 tbsp sherry vinegar
- 200g mixed radishes, cut into pieces
- 80g vegetarian feta, crumbled
- One small pack of dill, chopped
- 2 tbsp pumpkin seeds, toasted

Method
STEP 1

Preheat oven to 200C/180C fan/gas 6. Mix the oil and harissa, then toss the butternut squash and some spices in a large roasting pan. For 30 minutes, roast. Mix in the chickpeas and cook for another 20 minutes.

STEP 2

In the meantime, heat the sherry vinegar with a big pinch of sugar, a bit of salt, and 1 tbsp of water in a saucepan. Bring to a boil, turn off the heat and add the radishes. Mix and put to the side.

STEP 3

Put the butternut squash and chickpeas on a platter, mix most of the feta and dill, and then sprinkle the pickled radishes and their liquid on top. Add the rest of the feta, dill, and pumpkin seeds.

PRAWN & PINK GRAPEFRUIT NOODLE SALAD

Prep:25 mins

Serves 6

Ingredients

- 200g thin rice noodle (vermicelli)
- 12 cherry tomatoes, halved
- 1 tbsp fish sauce
- juice one lime
- 2 tsp palm sugar or soft brown sugar
- One large red chili, ½ diced, ½ sliced
- Two pink grapefruits, segmented
- ½ cucumber, peeled, deseeded, and thinly sliced
- Two carrots, cut into matchsticks
- Three spring onions, thinly sliced
- 400g cooked giant prawn
- large handful of mint leaves picked
- large handful of coriander leaves picked

Method
STEP 1

Break up the noodles and put them in a bowl. Cover the noodles with boiling water from the kettle. Leave to soak for 10 mins until tender. Drain the noodles, rinse them under cold running water, and then let them drain well.

STEP 2

We used the end of a rolling pin to lightly crush the cherry tomatoes in the same bowl. Mix the fish sauce, lime juice, sugar, and chili that has been cut up. Taste it to ensure it has the right amount of sweet, sour, and spicy.

STEP 3

Mix the noodles with the rest of the ingredients, except for the sliced chili. Season everything and give it a good stir. Put the noodle salad on six plates and sprinkle the chili on top before serving.

CHOPPED SALAD

Prep Time: 15 minutes

Yield: 8 servings

Ingredients

- One recipe for Homemade Italian Dressing
- 1 Romaine heart (3 cups)
- 5 cups of leafy lettuce
- One large shallot
- 1 English cucumber (2 cups of chopped)
- ½ cup of cherry tomatoes
- ½ cup of ripe green olives halved

- ½ cup of jarred sliced pepperoncini
- ¼ cup of Parmesan shavings
- ¼ tsp red pepper flakes,

Instructions

1. Make the Italian dressing at home.
2. Cut up the romaine and lettuce. Cut the shallot into thin slices. Peel a cucumber and cut it up. Tomatoes and olives should be cut in half.
3. The salad's ingredients, including the dressing, should be mixed and tossed to combine. If making ahead, store the salad and dressing separately in the fridge. Before serving, bring the dressing to room temperature.

SPINACH APPLE SALAD

Prep Time: 10 minutes

Yield: 4

Ingredients

- ½ cup of Glazed Walnuts
- One recipe Best Balsamic Dressing
- One apple
- One ripe pear
- 3 cups of baby spinach leaves
- 3 cups of baby mixed greens

Instructions

1. Make the Walnuts or Pecans with Glaze. (While they are cooking, put the rest of the salad together.
2. How to Make the Best Balsamic Dressing.
3. Core the apple and pear and slice them thinly.

4. Apples, pears, and walnuts should be on top of the greens. Pour the dressing over the salad and serve.

SIMPLE KALE SALAD

Prep Time: 15 minutes

Yield: 3 to 4 servings

Ingredients

- One large bunch of Tuscan kale (about 8 ounces)
- One very small
- ¼ tsp kosher salt
- 3 tbsp olive oil
- One lemon (3 to 4 tbsp juice, +zest)
- ¼ cup of freshly grated Parmesan cheese
- ⅛ tsp red pepper flakes
- Fresh ground black pepper
- Homemade croutons

Instructions

1. Wash the kale and let it dry. Then cut the kale leaves roughly and remove the stems.
2. Peel the garlic clove and chop it up. Sprinkle it with the kosher salt, then hold the blunt edge of the knife and scrape the sharp edge of the blade over the minced garlic while holding the knife at an angle and mashing the garlic into a paste.
3. Put the paste in the middle-sized bowl. Whisk together the olive oil, lemon juice, red pepper flakes, and freshly ground black pepper. Stir the Parmesan cheese into the dish.

4. Toss the kale leaves with the sauce. If you want, you can serve it with lemon zest and more Parmesan cheese on top. If you wish, serve with croutons you made yourself.

Notes

One bunch of kale makes a good-sized serving for four people. If you're feeding people who eat a lot, you might want to double the recipe.

PERFECT CAESAR SALAD

Prep Time: 10 minutes

Cook Time: 15 minutes

Ingredients
For the Caesar dressing (makes 1 cup)

- One medium garlic clove, minced
- ¼ cup of grated Parmesan cheese
- 2 tbsp lemon juice (1/2 lemon)
- ¼ cup of mayonnaise
- ½ cup of Greek yogurt
- 1 tbsp olive oil
- ½ tbsp Dijon mustard
- 1 tsp anchovy paste
- ¼ tsp every kosher salt and fresh ground black pepper

For the Caesar salad

- One recipe for Homemade Croutons
- Three romaine hearts
- ½ cup of Parmesan cheese shavings

Instructions

1. Make the Homemade Croutons, but instead of cutting the bread into cubes, tear it into pieces.
2. For the dressing, put all ingredients in a bowl and whisk them together. You can keep leftovers in the fridge for up to a week in a jar with a lid.
3. Tear the romaine leaves into pieces for the salad. Every salad should have shavings of Parmesan cheese, croutons, and a dressing on top.

Notes

Romaine's hearts are easy to find in the produce section, selling them in separate bags.

EASY ARUGULA SALAD

Prep Time: 10 minutes

Yield: 6 to 8

Ingredients

- ¾ cup of Parmesan cheese shavings
- One small shallot
- 8 cups of (5 ounces) baby arugula
- 2 tbsp extra virgin olive oil
- ¼ tsp kosher salt, +more to taste
- 1 ½ tbsp lemon juice + zest of ½ lemon

Instructions

1. If you need to, use a vegetable peeler to shave the Parmesan cheese. Slice the shallots thinly.
2. Put the baby arugula, olive oil, lemon zest, lemon juice, and kosher salt into a large bowl. Toss everything with your hands so that everything is evenly covered. Add the

shavings of Parmesan and the shallot and toss for a few seconds until everything is mixed together. Taste it and add more salt if you want.

Notes

For the quickest prep, buy a container of Parmesan shavings.

PERFECT ITALIAN SALAD

Prep Time: 15 minutes

Yield: 4 to 6

Ingredients

- 1/2 recipe Homemade Croutons
- One recipe for Homemade Italian Dressing
- 1 Romaine heart (3 cups)
- 5 cups of butter lettuce
- One handful of sliced red onion
- ½ cup of sliced cherry tomatoes
- ½ cup of sliced black olives
- ½ cup of jarred sliced pepperoncini
- ¼ cup of large Parmesan shavings (omit for vegan)

Instructions

1. Make the homemade croutons.
2. Make the Italian dressing.
3. Chop romaine and lettuce. Thinly slice the red onion. Slice the tomatoes in half.
4. Place the greens in bowls, then top with the vegetables, olives, pepperoncini, Parmesan shavings, and croutons, then drizzle with dressing. Or, you can place them all together in a large serving bowl and toss them with the dressing.

STRAWBERRY SPINACH SALAD

Prep Time: 15 minutes

Yield: 4

Ingredients
For the strawberry vinaigrette salad dressing (makes one ¼ cups of total)

- 1 ½ cups of sliced strawberries
- 2 tbsp maple syrup
- 2 tbsp apple cider vinegar
- ¼ cup of olive oil
- ¼ tsp kosher salt

For the strawberry spinach salad

- 1 cup of sliced strawberries
- One handful of thinly sliced red onion
- 5 cups of baby spinach leaves
- 3 cups of mixed greens
- ¼ cup of chopped pecans
- ¼ cup of feta cheese crumbles
- ½ cup of Strawberry Vinaigrette Salad Dressing

Instructions

1. To make the strawberry salad dressing, blend all ingredients in a standard blender, a small blender, or a stick blender until they are smooth. Most quickly, you can use an immersion or a small blender, but you can also use a regular blender. Just blend for a few minutes until everything is mixed well.
2. Get the ingredients for the salad ready: Cut the tops off of the strawberries and then cut them in half lengthwise. Cut

the red onion into thin slices (see the video for this method). Wash the spinach and mixed greens if you need to. If you have time, chop the pecans and toast them to make their taste better.

3. Serve by putting the greens on plates and adding all of the other ingredients on top. Then drizzle the strawberry vinaigrette salad dressing over the top (about 2 tbsp per serving). Keep the rest of the dressing in the fridge for up to a week.

CLASSIC WEDGE SALAD

Prep Time: 15 minutes

Yield: 4

Ingredients
For the salad

- One recipe for Blue Cheese Dressing
- One small head of iceberg lettuce
- 1 cup of cherry tomatoes, quartered
- Two chives, thinly sliced
- 3 tbsp blue cheese crumbles
- Smoky breadcrumbs for the garnish

For the smoky breadcrumbs

- 1 tbsp olive oil
- ½ cup of panko
- 1 tsp smoked paprika
- ½ tsp every onion powder and garlic powder
- 1/4 heaping tsp kosher salt

Instructions

1. Make the Blue Cheese Dressing.

2. Make the smoky breadcrumbs if using: Heat the olive oil in a small skillet over medium heat. In a small bowl, mix the panko with the smoked paprika, onion powder, garlic powder, and kosher salt. Add them to the skillet and toast, frequently stirring, until golden and crisp, about 2 to 3 minutes. Remove to a bowl.
3. Remove the outer leaves of the iceberg head, then slice it into wedges 4 for a small head, and 6 for a large head. Prep the chives and tomatoes.
4. To serve. Place a wedge on a plate. Top with dressing, tomatoes, chives, blue cheese crumbles, and smoky breadcrumbs. Serve immediately.

Notes

Not a fan of blue cheese? For a smokey flavor, make our Ranch Dressing and add 1/2 tsp of smoked paprika. Then crumble some feta cheese on top.

GOAT CHEESE SALAD WITH ARUGULA & APPLE

Prep Time: 15 minutes

Yield: 4

Ingredients

- One recipe for Balsamic Dressing
- One shallot
- 5 ounces (8 cups) baby arugula
- ¼ cup of pecans, roughly chopped
- 2 ounces soft goat cheese (chevre), crumbled
- Sea salt

Instructions

1. Make the dressing in a small bowl.

2. Cut the apple and shallot into thin slices.
3. Put the vegetables on a plate. On top, put the sliced shallot, apple, pecans, and soft goat cheese crumbles. Sprinkle with sea salt and drizzle with dressing.

Notes

Standard arugula has a taste that is much too spicy; look for small baby leaves like the ones in the photo. It comes in a package near the greens in the produce section, or you might be able to find it at your local farmer's market.

SIMPLE CARROT SALAD

Prep Time: 15 minutes

Yield: 4

Ingredients

- 1 tbsp white wine vinegar
- ½ tbsp Dijon mustard
- 1 tsp sugar or maple syrup
- ½ tsp kosher salt
- 3 tbsp olive oil
- 1 pound carrots, julienned (3 cups)
- Two green onions
- 3 tbsp chopped parsley

Instructions

1. In a medium bowl, whisk together the white wine vinegar, Dijon mustard, sugar or maple syrup, and kosher salt. Gradually mix in the olive oil.
2. Julienne the carrots using a julienne peeler, with the grating blade on a food processor, or using the large grate

holes of a box grater (this will do, but the pieces aren't as pretty).
3. Thinly slice the green onions. Finely chop the parsley.
4. Add all the vegetables to the bowl with the dressing and stir to combine. Serve immediately or refrigerate for up to 3 days.

EASY MEXICAN SALAD

Prep Time: 20 minutes

Yield: 4

Ingredients

- 3 Romaine hearts (8 cups of chopped)
- 2 cups of baby greens, like baby kale
- ¼ cup of sliced red onions
- ½ cup of cherry tomatoes
- 4 radishes
- 1 cup of frozen corn kernels, thawed
- One handful of roasted salted pepitas (pumpkin seeds)
- Dressing (pick one): Cilantro Lime Dressing, Creamy Cilantro Dressing, Chipotle Ranch, or Taco Salad Dressing (fastest)
- Add-ons: Crispy Tortilla Strips, crumbled feta or cotija cheese, chopped avocado, black beans, or chopped cucumber

Instructions

1. Make the Crispy Tortilla Strips if you want to use them. Or, you can make them the day before and keep them in an airtight container in the pantry until you're ready to eat.

2. To make the sauce: Cilantro Lime Dressing, Creamy Cilantro Dressing (shown), Chipotle Ranch, or Taco Salad Dressing (fastest!)
3. Cut up the veggies: Cut the romaine up. Cut the red onion into thin slices (follow the instructions at 1:30 of this video). Tomatoes should be cut in half. Cut the radishes into thin pieces. Let the corn warm up. Prepare any other vegetables that you want to add. Sprinkle a little salt on the tomatoes, radishes, and corn to season them lightly.
4. Serve: Put the greens on the plate, then the vegetables on top (and tortilla strips, if using). Put the dressing on top, and then serve. If making ahead, store the salad and sauce separately in the fridge. Before serving, bring the gravy to room temperature.

PEAR SALAD WITH PECANS

Ingredients
For the pear salad

- One ripe pear
- One shallot
- ½ cup of pecan pieces
- 8 cups of mixed baby greens
- ½ cup of pomegranate seeds
- ⅓ cup of gorgonzola cheese crumbles

For the dressing

- ¼ cup of granulated sugar
- ¼ cup of white vinegar
- 1 tsp dry mustard
- 1 tsp onion flakes
- ¼ tsp kosher salt
- ½ cup of grapeseed oil

- 1 tbsp poppy seeds

Instructions

1. To make the sauce: Whisk the granulated sugar, white vinegar, dry mustard, onion flakes, and kosher salt together in a medium bowl. Whisk in the grapeseed oil gradually, about 1 tbsp at a time, until you get a creamy emulsion. Add the poppy seeds with a whisk. Serve immediately or store in a container or jar with a lid until you're ready to eat.
2. Prepare the fresh food: Make thin slices of the pear. Cut the shallot into thin pieces. See How to Cut a Pomegranate for tips on how to get the seeds out of a pomegranate.
3. Toast the pecans if you have time: Put the nuts in a skillet with medium heat and no oil. Heat the nuts, shaking the pan and stirring them with a wooden spoon often, for about 4 to 5 minutes, until they smell good and are a little darker brown. Keep an eye on the nuts because they can easily burn. Take it off the heat immediately and put it on a plate to stop the cooking.
4. Serve: The greens should be put on a plate or platter on top; place slices of pear, shallot, toasted pecans, pomegranate seeds, and crumbled gorgonzola cheese. Drizzle with as much dressing as you want and serve.

ANTIPASTO SALAD

Prep Time: 10 minutes

Cook Time: 10 minutes

Ingredients

- 1/2 pound spiral pasta

- 1 cup of cherry tomatoes
- 1/4 medium red onion
- 2 cups of chopped romaine
- ¼ cup of chopped fresh basil
- One jarred roasted red pepper
- 1 cup of pitted olives
- 1 cup of artichoke quarters
- ½ cup of sliced pepperoncini
- 8 ounces mozzarella
- 2 tbsp white wine vinegar
- 1 tbsp Dijon mustard
- Two teaspoons of sugar or maple syrup
- 6 tbsp olive oil
- 1/2 to 1 tsp kosher salt
- 1 tbsp Italian seasoning

Instructions

1. Bring well-salted water to a boil in a pot. Boil the pasta until it is al dente. Start tasting it a few minutes before the package says to; you want it to be tender but still a little firm on the inside.
2. Cut the tomato halves in half. Cut the red onion into small cubes. Cut the romaine and fresh basil into pieces. Cut the roasted red pepper into thin slices.
3. Mix the cooked pasta, chopped vegetables, olives, artichoke quarters that have been rinsed, and pepperoncini in a large bowl (drained). Cut the mozzarella into cubes or pieces and add them.
4. Whisk the white wine vinegar, Dijon mustard, and sugar or maple syrup together in a small bowl. Whisk in the olive oil slowly.

5. Put the pasta and vegetables in a bowl. Pour the dressing on top, and then add the salt and Italian seasoning. Stir to mix. Taste and add more salt if you want.

QUINOA SALAD

Prep Time: 10 minutes

Cook Time: 15 minutes

Ingredients

- 1 cup of dry quinoa
- 1 cup of finely chopped curly parsley
- 1-pint cherry tomatoes, quartered
- 1 English cucumber, diced (peeled if using a standard cucumber)
- One red bell pepper, diced
- 1/2 to 1 bunch Tuscan kale
- Three green onions
- ¼ cup of minced shallot
- 1 tsp kosher salt, divided
- 1 tsp dried basil
- 2 tbsp red wine vinegar
- 2 tbsp Dijon mustard
- 1 tbsp honey or maple syrup
- ¼ cup of olive oil
- Fresh ground black pepper
- ⅓ cup of feta crumbles,

Instructions

1. To make the quinoa: Use a fine mesh strainer to rinse the quinoa, and then drain it all the way. Add 1 3/4 cups of water and 1/4 tsp of kosher salt. Bring to a boil, and then

turn down the heat. Cover the pot and let it cook on low heat for about 15 to 18 minutes, until all the water has been soaked up. Pull the quinoa back with a fork to see if there is still water. Turn off the heat and let the quinoa steam for 5 minutes with the lid on. Then, use a fork to fluff the quinoa. This step can be done the night before; put the quinoa in the fridge until you are ready to make the salad.

2. The quinoa should be at room temperature: If you want to make the salad right after you cook the quinoa, spread the quinoa out in an even layer on a baking sheet. Put it in the freezer for two to three minutes or until it has reached room temperature.

3. Chop the vegetables and add seasonings: Chop the parsley, tomatoes, cucumber, red pepper, Tuscan kale, and onions, as shown in the list of ingredients above. Mix them with the remaining 3/4 tsp of kosher salt and the dried basil in a large bowl.

4. To make the sauce: Whisk the honey or maple syrup, vinegar, and Dijon mustard together in a small bowl. Whisk in the olive oil slowly, one tbsp at a time, until all ingredients are mixed and an emulsion forms.

5. Blend the salad: Mix the quinoa, vegetables, and sauce. Eat right away, or let it sit for 30 minutes to 24 hours in a marinade (then taste and add additional salt if needed). Keeps in the fridge for 3 to 5 days.

Notes

Bunch sizes can vary; use half bunch if it's enormous or if you prefer a lower ratio of kale in your quinoa salad.

PERFECT POMEGRANATE SALAD

Ingredients

- 1 cup of pomegranate seeds
- One shallot
- 1 Granny Smith apple or Bosc pear
- ½ cup of toasted pecans
- One recipe for Apple Cider Vinegar Dressing
- 3 ounces (6 cups) of mixed greens
- 2 ounces soft goat cheese

Instructions

1. Cut and seed the pomegranate.
2. Thinly slice the shallot. Thinly slice the apple (toss it with 1 tsp lemon juice or vinegar if desired to prevent browning).
3. Toast the pecans (don't skip: this brings out the nutty flavor). Alternatively, make glazed pecans.
4. Make the Apple Cider Vinegar Dressing or Pomegranate Vinaigrette.
5. Place the greens on a platter. Top with the pomegranate seeds, sliced shallot, toasted pecans, and goat cheese or feta cheese crumbles. Toss with the desired amount of dressing to taste.

SWEET POTATO SALAD

Prep Time: 15 minutes

Cook Time: 25 minutes

Ingredients

- 2 pounds of sweet potatoes (about four medium)
- 2 tbsp extra-virgin olive oil

- 1 tsp garlic powder
- 1 tsp kosher salt
- Fresh ground black pepper
- 6 tbsp Honey Mustard Dressing (or Balsamic Dressing
- 2 cups of baby arugula
- 1/2 medium shallot, thinly sliced into half moons
- ¼ cup of dried cranberries
- ¼ cup of pepitas
- ¼ cup of feta or goat cheese crumbles

Instructions

1. Roast the sweet potatoes: Preheat the oven to 450 degrees Fahrenheit.
2. Dice the sweet potatoes into 3/4" cubes, leaving the skin on. In a large bowl, mix the sweet potatoes with olive oil, garlic powder, and kosher salt.
3. Line a baking sheet with parchment paper and place the sweet potatoes on top in an even layer. Bake for about 25 minutes until the cubes are tender and browned on the bottom. (You can prepare the roasted sweet potatoes and refrigerate them until serving: bring them to room temperature before making the salad, or reheat them in a 350-degree oven until slightly warmed.)
4. Meanwhile, make the Honey Mustard Dressing.
5. When ready to assemble the salad in a bowl, mix the roasted sweet potatoes with the baby arugula, shallot, cranberries, pepitas, feta or goat cheese crumbles, and 6 tbsp of the dressing. Mix, then serve. (Plated salad variation: Add 2 to 3 cups of mixed greens. Place the greens on plates, top with the potatoes, cranberries, shallot pepitas, and cheese, and drizzle with dressing.)

Notes

Be sure to buy baby arugula, which feels like feathers. Arugula that has grown up and is sold in bunches is way too spicy. Use any baby green instead, such as baby spinach or mixed greens.

CLASSIC CAPRESE SALAD

Ingredients

- 6 to 8 ripe heirloom tomatoes of different colors and sizes
- 4 ounces fresh mozzarella cheese or burrata cheese
- One handful of basil leaves
- Extra-virgin olive oil
- Balsamic reduction
- Sea salt
- Fresh ground pepper

Instructions

1. Slice the tomatoes and place them on a plate.
2. Top with torn or sliced mozzarella cheese and basil leaves. Drizzle with extra-virgin olive oil. If desired, drizzle with balsamic reduction. Top with sea salt and fresh ground pepper. Serve immediately.

CELERY SALAD WITH APPLES

Prep Time: 15 minutes

Yield: 6

Ingredients

- Eight celery ribs +½ cup of celery leaves
- One red apple
- 1 tbsp white wine vinegar
- ½ tbsp Dijon mustard
- 1 tsp maple syrup or sugar

- ½ tsp kosher salt
- 3 tbsp olive oil
- ¼ cup of shaved Parmesan cheese

Instructions

1. Thinly slice the celery ribs. Measure out the celery leaves. Thinly slice the red apple.
2. In a medium bowl, whisk together the white wine vinegar, Dijon mustard, maple syrup or sugar, and kosher salt. Gradually whisk in the olive oil one tbsp at a time.
3. In another bowl, toss the celery and celery leaves with the apple, dressing, and Parmesan cheese shavings. Serve immediately or refrigerate until serving. This tastes best the day of making, but you can refrigerate leftovers for a few days (refresh them with a bit of vinegar or salt if necessary).

BUTTER LETTUCE SALAD

Prep Time: 15 minutes

Yield: 4

Ingredients

- 5 ounces butter lettuce
- One shallot
- One handful of cherry tomatoes
- One handful of fresh chives
- ¼ cup of Italian panko
- ½ cup of Parmesan Peppercorn Dressing Parmesan shavings, for garnish

For the Parmesan Dressing

- ¼ cup of mayonnaise

- ½ cup of Greek yogurt
- ¼ cup of Parmesan cheese, finely grated
- 1 tbsp red wine vinegar
- ½ tbsp Dijon mustard
- ¼ tsp garlic powder
- ½ tsp every kosher salt and fresh ground black pepper
- 1 tbsp water

Instructions

1. Wash the lettuce and let it dry (a salad spinner does quick work). Then break it apart.
2. Cut the shallot into thin slices. Cut the cherry tomatoes into quarters or delicate pieces, and do the same with the radishes. Chop the chives very small.
3. To make the Parmesan dressing, whisk together the mayonnaise, Greek yogurt, grated Parmesan cheese, red wine vinegar, Dijon mustard, garlic powder, salt, black pepper, and water until a creamy dressing forms.
4. Put the butter lettuce on salad plates or a large platter. Sliced tomatoes or radishes, shallots, chives, and shavings of Parmesan cheese go on top. Drizzle with about a half cup of the dressing and sprinkle with Italian panko.

Notes

Panko is a mixture of breadcrumbs made in Japan. It is lighter and airier than regular breadcrumbs. It has a crunchy texture that makes salads taste better (breadcrumbs are much finer with almost a sand-like surface). "Italian" means that you add herbs and salt. Your local grocery store should have no trouble stocking Italian or plain panko (often, they also sell gluten-free). If you only have plain panko, you can spice it with: half a cup of panko, an eighth of a tsp of kosher salt, and half a tbsp of Italian seasoning.

ROMAINE LETTUCE SALAD WITH GREEN GODDESS

Ingredients

- Two romaine hearts (about 8 cups of chopped)
- Two radishes, thinly sliced
- One shallot, thinly sliced
- ½ cup of Green Goddess Dressing
- ¼ cup of Italian panko
- Parmesan shavings, for garnish

Instructions

1. Chop the romaine hearts. Thinly slice the radishes and shallot.
2. Make the Green Goddess Dressing.
3. Place the romaine on salad plates or a large platter. Top with the sliced radishes, shallot, and Parmesan cheese shavings. Drizzle with dressing and sprinkle with Italian panko.

Notes

Panko is a mixture of breadcrumbs made in Japan. It is lighter and airier than regular breadcrumbs. It has a crunchy texture that makes salads taste better (breadcrumbs are much finer with almost a sand-like texture). "Italian" means that you add herbs and salt. Your local grocery store should have no trouble stocking Italian or plain panko (often, they also sell gluten-free). If you only have plain panko, you can spice it by half a cup of panko, an eighth of a tsp of kosher salt, and half a tbsp of Italian seasoning.

HEARTY FARRO SALAD

Prep Time: 10 minutes

Cook Time: 20 minutes

Ingredients

- 1 cup of dry farro
- 1 tsp kosher salt, divided
- One shallot, minced
- One small garlic clove, minced
- 1 cup of cherry tomatoes, halved or quartered
- 4 ounces button
- One carrot, peeled and thinly sliced
- ¼ cup of chopped fresh herbs
- 2 cups of baby arugula
- ½ cup of Manchego cheese, cut into chunks
- 2 tbsp lemon juice
- 1 tsp Dijon mustard
- ½ tsp dried oregano
- 3 tbsp olive oil

Instructions

1. To cook the farro, rinse it in a fine mesh strainer with cold water. Put the farro, 3 cups of water, and 1/2 tsp of kosher salt in a large saucepan and bring it to a boil. Reduce the heat to a simmer, cover, and cook until the grains are soft, about 15 to 20 minutes for pearled farro and 25 to 30 minutes for semi-pearled farro. Try a grain to see if it is smooth to the taste (if the package is unmarked, just cook until tender). Remove any extra water. Mix in the extra 14 tsp of salt. Put them in a single layer on a baking sheet and put them in the freezer for 3

minutes until they are at room temperature. (This step can be done up to two days ahead; put the farro in the fridge until you're ready to make the salad.)

2. Set up the vegetables: In the meantime, chop the shallot, garlic, cherry tomatoes, mushrooms, carrot, and fresh herbs, as shown in the list of ingredients above. Add the vegetables, baby arugula, cheese, and farro to a large bowl.

3. To make the sauce: Whisk the lemon juice, Dijon mustard, oregano, and 1/4 tsp of kosher salt together in a medium bowl. Whisk in the olive oil gradually, one tbsp at a time, until the mixture is smooth.

4. To serve, pour the dressing over the farro and vegetables and stir. Taste it and if you want, add another pinch or two of salt.

CLASSIC CORN SALAD

Prep Time: 20 minutes

Cook Time: 5 minutes

Ingredients

- Six cobs of corn (about 5 cups of kernels,
- ½ pint (1 cup) cherry tomatoes
- ½ cup of diced red onion
- ⅓ cup of roughly chopped fresh basil
- 2 tbsp apple cider vinegar
- 2 tbsp olive oil
- ¼ tsp garlic powder
- ¼ tsp chili powder
- ½ tsp kosher salt
- Fresh ground black pepper

- ½ cup of feta cheese crumbles for garnish

Instructions

1. Cook the corn: Bring a large pot of water to a boil. (This takes about 15 to 20 minutes, so plan accordingly.) Shuck the corn, removing the silk. When the water is boiling, place the corn cobs in the pot. Boil covered for 4 minutes, until bright yellow. Run under cool water until cool enough to touch. (Alternate method: Roast the corn in the oven or use canned corn.)
2. Cut the corn: Find a bundt pan, large rimmed baking sheet, or pan. Place the corn into the hole in the bundt pan or hold the corn vertically inside the baking sheet, then use a chef's knife to slice down and remove the corn from the cob (the sides of the pan catch the kernels that fly when cutting; more details here.)
3. Chop the vegetables: Meanwhile, dice the cherry tomatoes. Finely chop the red onion. Chop the basil.
4. Mix in the dressing: In a large bowl, mix all vegetables with the apple cider vinegar, olive oil, garlic powder, chili powder, salt, fresh ground black pepper to taste, and optional feta crumbles. Stores refrigerated for up to 3 days.

GREEK ORZO SALAD RECIPE

Prep Time: 15 minutes

Cook Time: 10 minutes

Ingredients

- 8 ounces orzo pasta (1 ¼ cup of dry)
- 1 cup of canned chickpeas, drained and rinsed
- 1/2 lemon, juice, and zest (about 2 tbsp juice)

- ¼ cup of minced shallot or red onion
- 1/2 English cucumber (2 cups of diced, or substitute a peeled standard cucumber)
- Two roasted red peppers from a jar or ½ fresh red bell pepper (½ cup of diced)
- ⅓ cup of chopped dill, +more for garnish
- ⅓ cup of chopped mint
- 2 tbsp white wine vinegar
- 3 tbsp extra-virgin olive oil
- ½ tsp Dijon mustard
- 1 tsp dried oregano
- ½ cup of feta cheese crumbles
- ⅓ cup of Kalamata olives halved
- Black pepper

Instructions

1. Prepare the orzo according to the package instructions. Taste the orzo a few minutes before completion to ensure it's 'all dented (chewy, but with a bit of firmness in the center). When it's done, drain it and then rinse it under cold water until it comes to room temperature.
2. Place the chickpeas in a bowl with lemon zest, lemon juice, and ¼ tsp kosher salt.
3. Mince the red onion, then place it in a bowl with water (this helps to remove the sharp onion taste). Dice the cucumber. Dice the roasted red pepper. Chop the herbs.
4. Stir together the orzo, chickpeas, and bowl of lemon juice, red onion, cucumber, red pepper, dill, mint, white wine vinegar, olive oil, Dijon mustard, oregano, feta crumbles, black olives, and several grinds of black pepper. Taste and, if necessary, season with more kosher salt.

SPRING MIX SALAD

Ingredients

- 8 cups of spring mix salad greens
- One large carrot
- 1/4 small red onion or one shallot
- ¼ cup of feta cheese crumbles
- ¼ cup of chopped pecans, walnuts, almonds
- One apple, sliced or diced
- Balsamic Vinaigrette, Dijon Dressing, Orange Vinaigrette, Ginger Dressing, or Poppy Seed Dressing

Instructions

1. Make the dressing: Try Balsamic Vinaigrette, Dijon Dressing, Orange Vinaigrette, or Poppy Seed Dressing.
2. Prepare the vegetables: Slice the onion and, if desired, soak it in cold water while preparing the rest of the salad (to remove the bite). Or, slice the shallot into rings. Peel the carrot into ribbons or julienne it. Chop the nuts.
3. Serve: Place the spring mix greens on a platter or salad plate, and top with carrots, onion, feta crumbles, and chopped nuts. Drizzle with dressing and serve (about 1 to 1 ½ tbsp per serving).

FENNEL ORANGE SALAD

Prep Time: 20 minutes

Yield: 4

Ingredients

- 1/2 recipe Citrus Vinaigrette
- One fennel bulb
- One large shallot

- Two small oranges: blood orange
- 2 tbsp chopped pistachios
- 5 ounces baby mixed greens (about 5 cups)

Instructions

1. Make the citrus dressing.
2. Cut the fennel and shallot into thin slices. Save a few fronds (the feathery green parts on top of the stalk) if you want to use them as a garnish.
3. Follow How to Cut an Orange to cut an orange into pieces or "supremes."
4. Put the greens on a plate to serve. Oranges, fennel, shallots, and chopped pistachios should be put on top (and fennel fronds if desired). Add the dressing, and then serve.

Notes

You can use any type you want! It's nice to use a variety of greens so that the texture and taste will be different. If you use baby kale, arugula, or spinach, make sure to mix them with other greens that aren't as strong. Mixed lettuces are also lovely because they have a nice crunch and are refreshing.

LENTIL SALAD WITH FETA

Prep Time: 15 minutes

Cook Time: 15 minutes

Ingredients
For the lentils

- 1 pound black beluga lentils or French lentils
- 1-quart vegetable broth+ 2 cups of water
- 1 tsp kosher salt

- 1 tsp dried thyme
- ½ tsp garlic powder

For the lentil salad

- 2 tbsp red wine vinegar
- 2 tbsp lemon juice + zest of 1 lemon
- 1 tsp Dijon mustard
- ½ tsp onion powder
- 1 tsp dried oregano
- 6 tbsp olive oil
- One shallot
- One red pepper
- 2 tbsp chopped fresh mint
- ½ tsp kosher salt + fresh ground pepper
- 1 cup of baby arugula, +more to serve
- 1 cup of feta cheese crumbles, +more for garnish
- ½ cup of pistachios, +more for garnish
- Three radishes for garnish

Instructions

1. For the lentils, put the broth, water, kosher salt, thyme, and garlic powder in a large saucepan or deep skillet. Simmer the lentils for about 15 to 20 minutes until they are soft. Drain excess liquid.
2. To make the sauce: Whisk the red wine vinegar, lemon juice, lemon zest, Dijon mustard, onion powder, and oregano together in a large bowl. Mix in the olive oil one tbsp at a time until the mixture is smooth and creamy.
3. Cut up the vegetables: Cut the shallot into thin slices. Cut the red pepper into thin slices, and then cut every slice in half to make pieces that are about 2 inches long. If you want to use them, chop them.

4. Put the salad together: Put the lentils and dressing in the large bowl. Mix in the shallot, pepper, herbs, baby arugula, feta cheese, and pistachios. Mix in the 1/2 tsp of kosher salt and the freshly ground pepper.

5. Serve: If desired, serve over arugula. Add thinly sliced radishes and a sprinkle of feta and pistachios to the top. Any leftovers can be kept in the fridge for up to 4 days. If you want to make this for lunch, leave out the pistachios. It keeps well and tastes even better the next day.

NICOISE SALAD

Prep Time: 25 minutes

Cook Time: 15 minutes

Ingredients

- Eight eggs
- 1 1/2 pounds of baby red potatoes
- 1 pound of fresh green beans
- One small shallot (2 tbsp minced)
- 2 tbsp white wine vinegar
- ¾ tsp kosher salt, divided
- 2 tbsp capers
- ½ tbsp fresh parsley
- 7 tbsp olive oil, divided
- ½ cup of Nicoise or Kalamata olives
- 1-pint cherry tomatoes or one large tomato
- Two cans of tuna, packed in oil or water
- One head of Bibb lettuce
- 3 tbsp lemon juice
- 1 tbsp Dijon mustard
- One small garlic clove, minced

Instructions

1. Cook the hard-boiled eggs: Follow the directions for Hard Boiled Eggs or Steamed Hard Boiled Eggs, or do this step ahead of time and put it in the fridge.
2. Boil the beans and potatoes: Add 1 tbsp of kosher salt to a large pot of cold water. Bring to a boil, then add the whole potatoes. Once the water is boiling, let it cook for 8 to 12 minutes, or until the food is soft enough to cut with a fork.
3. Cook the beans: Cut the beans' ends off. Bring a separate pot of water and 12 tbsp salt to a boil. Boil the beans for about 5 minutes until they are soft but bright green. Get a big bowl of ice water ready (or use the same one for the hard-boiled eggs). When the beans are soft, take them out of the boiling water and put them in the ice bath with tongs. Take out the beans and dry them with a towel. Mix them with a few pinches of salt and freshly ground pepper.
4. To finish the potatoes, chop the shallot while the potatoes are cooking. Drain the potatoes when they are done. When they are cool enough to touch, cut them into pieces that are easy to eat. Put them in a bowl and gently stir in the minced shallot, white wine vinegar, 1/2 tsp kosher salt, and 1/4 cup warm water. Let it sit for 5 minutes, stirring it gently every so often. Then, add the capers, chopped parsley, 1 tbsp of olive oil, and a few grinds of black pepper. Taste it and add more salt if you think it needs it.
5. To make the sauce: Mix the lemon juice, Dijon mustard, minced garlic, and 1/4 tsp of kosher salt in a medium bowl with a whisk. Whisk in the olive oil slowly, one tbsp at a time, until the mixture is smooth and creamy.

6. Put together the salad: Cut the tomatoes into wedges (or cut cherry tomatoes in half) and sprinkle with kosher salt.
7. Making the tuna: With a fork, break up the tuna that has been drained. If they aren't already packed in oil, add a few pinches of salt and a drizzle of olive oil.
8. Serve: To serve, put the Bibb lettuce leaves in large shallow bowls or on large plates. On top, put the potatoes, green beans, hard-boiled eggs, tomatoes, tuna, and olives. Add the dressing, and then serve.

FRISEE SALAD

Prep Time: 15 minutes

Yield: 4

Ingredients
For the frisee salad

- One large or 2 to 3 small heads frisee
- One orange, +zest
- One shallot
- 1 ounce Manchego cheese
- 2 tbsp sliced almonds
- One handful of fresh mint leaves,

For the dressing (makes ½ cup; use 3 to 4 tbsps)

- 2 tbsp white wine vinegar
- 1 tbsp Dijon mustard
- 1 tbsp maple syrup or honey
- ¼ tsp kosher salt
- 6 tbsp olive oil
- Fresh ground black pepper

Instructions

1. Use a salad spinner or a clean towel to wash and dry the frisée. Cut or tear the frisee into small pieces.
2. Juice half of the orange. Then cut the orange into pieces, just like it says in How to Cut an Orange.
3. Cut the shallot into thin slices. The Manchego cheese should be cut into pieces.
4. Whisk the white wine vinegar, Dijon, maple syrup, or honey, and salt together in a medium bowl. Mix in the oil one tbsp at a time with a whisk until you have a creamy dressing. Add a few grinds of black pepper that have just been ground. Serve immediately or put in the fridge for up to two weeks (bring to room temperature before serving).
5. When ready to serve the salad, put the greens on a big platter or separate plates. Orange slices, shallot, cheese, sliced almonds, orange zest, and mint leaves decorate the dish. Drizzle on 3 to 4 tbsp of the dressing, depending on how you like it.

Notes

Sizes sold in stores vary greatly depending on how old the plant is. You can see a big head of frisee in the picture above. If the charges are small, you may need two or three. Total, there should be about 6 cups of greens.

ENDIVE SALAD WITH PARMESAN & ORANGE

Ingredients

- 3 heads Belgian endive
- ½ cup of thinly sliced radicchio
- Two oranges, +zest
- 2 tbsp sliced almonds

- Pecorino or Parmesan cheese shaved
- ¼ cup of Red Wine Vinaigrette

Instructions

1. Cut off the bottom 1/2-inch of the endives. Cut the leaves in half lengthwise, leaving most smaller leaves whole. Rinse the leaves and blot them dry with a towel or place them in a salad spinner to dry.
2. Zest one orange. Then cut both of the oranges into segments.
3. Make the Red Wine Vinaigrette.
4. Place the endive leaves on a large plate or platter or individual plates. Top with the sliced radicchio, orange zest, slices, sliced almonds, and shavings of Pecorino or Parmesan cheese. Top with the red wine vinaigrette.

WHITE BEAN SALAD

Ingredients

- One can of navy beans
- ½ cup of diced red bell pepper
- 1 tbsp finely chopped red onion or shallot
- 2 tbsp finely chopped parsley
- 1/2 to 1 tbsp olive oil
- 1/2 to 1 tbsp red wine vinegar
- ½ tbsp Dijon mustard
- ¼ tsp kosher salt
- Fresh ground black pepper
- 2 tbsp feta cheese (omit for vegan)

Instructions

1. Drain and rinse the beans.

2. Dice the bell pepper. Mince the red onion, and chop the parsley.
3. In a bowl, mix all ingredients (if you're eating right away, use the ½ tbsp oil and vinegar; if making to refrigerate or for a party where it will sit out, use 1 tbsp). Taste and add additional salt if desired. Saves up to 3 days refrigerated; taste and add extra salt, olive oil, and vinegar after storage.

EASY VEGETABLE SALAD

Prep Time: 20 minutes

Yield: 4

Ingredients

- One large red bell pepper (1 ½ cups of small diced)
- 1/2 red onion (½ cup of diced)
- 1/2 English cucumber
- Two heads of broccoli (2 cups of tiny florets)
- 1/2 head cauliflower (2 cups of small florets)
- Two green onions
- ¼ cup of feta cheese crumbles
- 2 tbsp olive oil
- 2 tbsp red wine vinegar
- 1 tbsp Dijon mustard
- ¼ tsp every garlic powder and onion powder
- ¾ tsp kosher salt
- Fresh ground black pepper

Instructions

1. Cut the vegetables up the way we said above and put them in a big bowl. (Make sure the broccoli and cauliflower are cut into small florets.)
2. Mix in the olive oil, red wine vinegar, Dijon mustard, garlic powder, onion powder, salt, and pepper. Taste and add more salt if you want. You can eat it immediately or put it in the fridge for up to 3 days.

Notes

Or, customize this vegetable salad by using 7 to 8 cups of bite-size chopped vegetables of your choosing. If you're serving ravenous eaters or want a large batch, make a double recipe: click the 2x button above.

Suppose you use a standard cucumber, peel, and seed it. English cucumber has a fragile, delicate skin that doesn't need to be peeled and imperceptible seeds.

FENNEL SALAD WITH PARMESAN

Ingredients

- Two heads of fennel (4 to 5 cups of sliced), +fennel fronds
- One apple
- ¼ cup of shaved Parmesan cheese (omit for vegan)
- 2 tbsp lemon juice, +zest of ½ lemon
- 1 tbsp olive oil
- ¼ tsp kosher salt
- Fresh ground black pepper

Instructions

1. Cut off the fennel stalks with a large chef's knife and save them for the garnish. Then cut the fennel's root end off.

Take off and throw away any tough layers outside the fennel. Cut the fennel bulb down the middle. Place it on the side where it was cut and make skinny half-moon slices that run parallel to the root end. Read more at How to Cut Fennel. If you have a mandolin, you can also use it to cut skinny slices.

2. Cut the apple into thin slices. Put the apple and fennel slices in a medium bowl. Then, use a vegetable peeler to make thin shavings of Parmesan cheese and add them to the bowl.

3. Add the lemon juice, peel, olive oil, kosher salt, and freshly ground black pepper. With your fingers, pull off the wispy parts (the fronds) and roughly tear them until you have enough for about 2 to 3 tbsps. Put the pieces in the bowl.

4. Be careful not to break the apple slices as you gently mix the salad with your hands until it is evenly coated. Enjoy immediately or refrigerate until serving. Stores in the fridge for up to 3 days. To bring out the flavors again, add a pinch of salt and a bit of lemon juice or zest.

BUTTERNUT SQUASH SALAD

Prep Time: 15 minutes

Cook Time: 30 minutes

Ingredients
For the butternut squash salad

- One recipe Roasted Butternut Squash
- 8 cups of mixed greens
- One red apple, diced
- ¼ cup of dried cranberries

- ¼ cup of feta cheese or goat cheese crumbles (omit for vegan)
- 3 tbsp chopped pecans

For the orange vinaigrette (makes ¾ cup; use approximately 6 tbsp for four servings)

- 2 tbsp white wine vinegar
- 1 tbsp Dijon mustard
- 1 tbsp orange zest
- 2 tbsp honey
- ¼ tsp kosher salt
- ½ cup of olive oil

Instructions

1. Roast the squash: Make the Roasted Butternut Squash, following the instructions in that recipe. We suggest making this portion in advance; store the roasted squash refrigerated until ready to use and bring to room temperature before serving.
2. Make the dressing: In a medium bowl, whisk together the white wine vinegar, Dijon mustard, orange zest, honey, and kosher salt. Gradually whisk in the olive oil 1 tbsp until a creamy dressing forms. (Store leftovers refrigerated and bring to room temperature before serving.
3. Serve the salad: Add greens to a platter or individual salad plates, and top with the roasted squash, diced apple, cranberries, cheese crumbles, and chopped pecans. Drizzle with the desired amount of dressing (use approximately 6 tbsp for four servings; store the remaining sauce refrigerated.

BEST CLASSIC POTATO SALAD

Prep Time: 20 minutes

Cook Time: 10 minutes

Ingredients

- 3 pounds Yukon gold potatoes
- 3 tbsp white wine vinegar, divided
- One ¼ tsp kosher salt, divided
- Three large celery stalks
- Five green onions, thinly sliced in both white and green portions
- ¼ cup of red onion, minced
- 2 tbsp chopped fresh dill
- ½ cup of sweet pickle relish
- ½ cup of mayonnaise
- ½ cup of Greek yogurt or sour cream
- 3 tbsp yellow mustard
- 1 tsp celery seed

Instructions

1. Boil the potatoes: Quarter the potatoes, keeping the skins on. Place them in a large saucepan filled with cold water. Bring it to a boil and cook for 8 to 12 minutes until tender when pricked with a fork. Drain and rinse the potatoes under cold water. Allow to cool slightly, peel the skins off with your fingers, and cut the potatoes into bite-sized pieces. Place the potatoes into a bowl and sprinkle with 2 tbsp of the white wine vinegar and ½ tsp of kosher salt. Mix and let stand 5 minutes.

2. Meanwhile, prep the salad: Slice the celery stalks in half lengthwise, then thinly slice them. Thinly slice the green onions. Mince the red onion. Chop the dill.

3. In a large bowl, mix the mayonnaise, Greek yogurt or sour cream, yellow mustard, Dijon mustard, celery seed, 1 tbsp of the white wine vinegar, ¾ of the tsp kosher salt, and plenty of fresh ground pepper. Add the potatoes, celery, green onion, red onion, and sweet pickle relish and stir until thoroughly combined. For best results, chill 2 hours before serving. Stores 5 days refrigerated.

Notes

The variety here is essential: use Yukon gold or gold potatoes for best results.

EASY CABBAGE SALAD

Ingredients

- 2 tbsp fresh lemon juice
- 2 tbsp olive oil
- ½ tbsp Dijon mustard
- One medium-head green cabbage
- ¾ tsp kosher salt
- 2 tbsp finely chopped mint leaves

Instructions

1. Mix the lemon juice, olive oil, and Dijon mustard in a large bowl with a whisk.
2. Cut the cabbage up. Chop the mint up very small. Put them in the bowl and toss them with the dressing.

EASY BLACK BEAN SALAD

Prep Time: 15 minutes

Cook Time: 15 minutes

Ingredients

- 2 cups of water
- 1 cup of uncooked long grain rice
- 15-ounce can of black beans, rinsed and drained
- One red bell pepper
- One yellow bell pepper
- Five green onions
- ¼ cup of olive oil
- ¼ cup of apple cider vinegar
- 1 tbsp Dijon mustard
- 1 tsp ground cumin
- One large garlic clove
- ¾ tsp kosher salt
- ¼ tsp freshly ground black pepper

Instructions

1. Pour 2 cups of water into a medium saucepan. Bring to a boil, add the uncooked rice, stir to combine, and return to a spot. Cover the pan, and reduce heat as low as possible. Simmer without opening the lid for 15 minutes until the rice is tender and the water is absorbed. (Or, use our Stovetop White Rice, Stovetop Brown Rice, or Instant Pot Rice methods.)
2. Finely chop the peppers. Thinly slice the green onions. Mince the garlic.

3. In a large mixing bowl, mix the cooked rice, black beans, chopped red and yellow peppers, and scallions, and toss to combine.
4. In a small bowl or measuring cup, mix the olive oil, apple cider vinegar, mustard, cumin, garlic, salt, and black pepper; whisk thoroughly to combine, then pour over the rice mixture. Toss gently to coat, then serve immediately or keep refrigerated for up to 3 days.

Notes

Reprinted with permission from Husbands That Cook: More Than 120 Irresistible Vegetarian Recipes and Tales from Our Tiny Kitchen by Ryan Alvarez and Adam Merrin

ASPARAGUS SALAD WITH FETA

Prep Time: 15 minutes

Cook Time: 5 minutes

Ingredients

- One recipe Sauteed Asparagus
- 1/4 red onion
- Three radishes
- One recipe for Dijon Mustard Dressing
- ⅓ cup of feta cheese crumbles
- Two bunches of salad greens, including romaine lettuce (about 8 cups)
- Lemon zest, for garnish (using the lemon from the asparagus recipe)
- turn it into a main dish salad by adding cooked quinoa!

Instructions

1. Thinly slice the red onion into slivers. Place them in a bowl of water while you prepare the salad, then drain before using (this mellows the strong flavor). Thinly slice the radishes.
2. Make the Sauteed Asparagus. Remove to a bowl until serving.
3. Make the Dijon Mustard Dressing.
4. To serve, clean, and dry the salad greens as necessary. Place the greens on serving plates, then top with sauteed asparagus, red onion, radishes, feta cheese crumbles, and lemon zest. Drizzle with dressing and serve.

SIMPLE CITRUS SALAD

Ingredients

- Two small grapefruit
- One navel orange
- Two small blood oranges
- One small shallot
- 1 tbsp white wine vinegar
- 1 tsp Dijon mustard
- 1 tsp maple syrup
- Pinch kosher salt
- 3 tbsp olive oil
- Fresh mint, for garnish
- Fresh ground pepper, for garnish
- Finely crushed pistachios for garnish

Instructions

1. Cut off the peel of the grapefruit and oranges: slice off the ends, then angle your knife and follow the curve to

remove the peels (follow Steps 1 & 2 of How to Cut an Orange). Slice the citrus into rings.

2. Thinly slice the shallot into thin rings.
3. In a medium bowl, stir together the white wine vinegar, Dijon mustard, maple syrup, and one pinch of kosher salt. Then gradually whisk in the olive oil 1 tbsp until creamy.
4. Arrange the citrus and shallots on a platter or serving plates. Drizzle with vinaigrette. Top with torn mint leaves and fresh ground pepper. If desired, top with finely crushed pistachios.

SIMPLE AVOCADO SALAD

Ingredients

- Two avocados
- 1-pint cherry tomatoes, multi-colored
- 1/2 red onion
- 2 tbsp chopped basil, cilantro
- One small garlic clove
- 2 tbsp fresh lemon juice
- 1 tbsp Dijon mustard
- ½ tsp kosher salt
- ¼ cup of olive oil
- New ground black pepper, to taste

Instructions

1. Chopped up the avocados. Cut the tomato halves in half. Make thin slices of the red onion. Cut the herbs up. Chopped up the garlic.
2. Mix the lemon juice, Dijon mustard, and kosher salt in a large bowl with a whisk. Whisk in the olive oil slowly.

3. Mix gently with the chopped avocado, tomato, red onion, and herbs. Salad tastes best when it's made fresh. Leftovers are stored refrigerated for one day.

SIMPLE CHICKPEA SALAD

Ingredients

- 15-ounce can chickpeas
- ¼ cup of bell pepper, diced
- ¼ cup of English cucumber, chopped
- ½ tbsp olive oil
- ½ tbsp red wine vinegar
- ½ tsp kosher salt
- ½ tsp smoked paprika
- Fresh ground pepper
- One pinch of celery seed or freshly torn herbs (parsley, dill, basil, etc.)

Instructions

1. Drain and rinse the chickpeas.
2. Dice the bell pepper. Chop the cucumber (peel it if you're using a standard cucumber; English cucumber doesn't need to be peeled).
3. In a bowl, mix all ingredients. Taste and add salt as desired.

BEET SALAD WITH GOAT CHEESE

Prep Time: 15 minutes

Cook Time: 15 minutes

Ingredients

- Four medium beets

- One recipe for Best Balsamic Vinaigrette
- One shallot
- 5 ounces (8 cups) of baby greens
- 2 ounces soft goat cheese
- ¼ cup of roasted salted pistachios, roughly chopped

Instructions

1. Cook the beets: Use our Oven Roasted Beets or Instant Pot Beets method.
2. Slice the beets: Slice the beets into wedges. Take proper precautions as beet juice stains easily).
3. Make the dressing: In a medium bowl, make the Best Balsamic Vinaigrette.
4. Toss the beets with the sauce (optional): Place the beets in the bowl with the sauce and stir. The beets will change the color of the sauce to a bright pink color and infuse a little sweetness. If you'd rather keep the balsamic vinaigrette color, you can skip this step.
5. Assemble the salad: Thinly slice the shallot. Place the greens on a plate. Remove the beets from the dressing bowl and place them on top. Add crumbles of goat cheese, shallot, and chopped pistachios. Drizzle with dressing and serve.

WATERMELON CUCUMBER SALAD

Ingredients

- 8 cups of cubed ripe seedless watermelon (1 8-pound watermelon)
- Two organic mini cucumbers or ½ English cucumber (1 cup of sliced)
- 2 ounces Feta cheese crumbles
- Zest of 1/2 lemon

- Four basil leaves
- Sea salt, for garnish

Instructions

1. Chop the watermelon into cubes. Slice the cucumbers (if using an English cucumber, slice it into half moons). Chop the basil. Zest the lemon.
2. Arrange the watermelon and cucumbers on a platter. Sprinkle with feta crumbles, lemon zest, and sea salt. Taste and adjust flavors as desired. Serve immediately. If making ahead, refrigerate the cubed watermelon separately: it releases a lot of water after it is cut. Then assemble the salad directly before serving.

SMOKED SALMON SALAD

Ingredients
For the salad

- 10 ounces of greens (2 to 3 cups per plate)
- 8 ounces smoked salmon
- 4 to 6 large sprigs of fresh dill, torn into pieces
- 4 ounces soft goat cheese
- ¼ cup of red onion slices
- Sesame seeds, for the garnish

For the vinaigrette dressing

- 2 tbsp white wine vinegar
- 1 tbsp Dijon mustard
- 1 tsp honey
- ¼ tsp kosher salt
- Fresh ground black pepper
- 6 tbsp olive oil
- 2 tbsp finely minced shallot (1/2 medium shallot)

Instructions

1. To make the vinaigrette dressing, mix the white wine vinegar, Dijon mustard, honey, kosher salt, and freshly ground black pepper in a medium bowl with a whisk. Whisk in the olive oil a tbsp at a time until a creamy emulsion forms. Keep in the fridge and let it come to room temperature before serving (at least two weeks).
2. Make the smoked salmon salad: Put the vegetables on a plate. Add smoked salmon pieces, torn dill, dollops of goat cheese, and thinly sliced red onions. Add the dressing, and then serve.

BLACK BEAN AND CORN SALAD

Prep Time: 5 minutes

Yield: 4

Ingredients

- 15-ounce can of black beans
- 15-ounce can corn
- 1 cup of fresh pico de gallo, aka fresh salsa
- ½ tsp kosher salt
- 1 tsp olive oil
- Fresh cilantro, if desired (for garnish)

Instructions

1. Drain and rinse the black beans. Drain the corn. In a bowl, mix them with the pico de gallo, salt, and olive oil.
2. If desired, add torn cilantro. Serve immediately with a slotted spoon as a side salad, in a rice bowl, in tacos, or as a dip with tortilla chips.

Notes

For a party size, double the ingredients.

You'll find this packaged in the refrigerated section at your local grocery: it may be labeled pico de gallo or fresh salsa. If you can't find it, make homemade Pico de Gallo.

EASY TORTELLINI SALAD

Prep Time: 15 minutes

Cook Time: 5 minutes

Ingredients

- 18 ounces refrigerated cheese tortelloni
- 2 ½ ounces (2 cups) baby spinach or chopped spinach
- One handful of fresh basil leaves, roughly chopped (recommended: add another handful chopped fresh dill)
- 14-ounce can (8.5-ounce dry weight) quartered artichokes, roughly chopped
- 1-pint cherry tomatoes, sliced in half
- ¼ cup of white wine vinegar
- 1 tbsp granulated sugar
- ½ tsp of every dried dill and garlic powder
- 1 tsp kosher salt, +more to taste
- Fresh ground black pepper
- ¼ cup of olive oil
- ¼ cup of neutral oil
- ¾ cup of shredded Parmesan cheese

Instructions

1. Start a large pot of well-salted water to boil. Boil the pasta until al dente according to the package instructions

(usually around 2 minutes). Drain the pasta and run cool water over it until it's warm.

2. Meanwhile, while the pasta cooks, chop the spinach, basil, and artichoke hearts and slice the tomatoes. In a large bowl, whisk together the vinegar, sugar, dried dill, garlic powder, kosher salt, and fresh ground black pepper. Then whisk in the olive oil and neutral oil.

3. Once the pasta is done, add it to the large bowl of dressing and toss with the chopped vegetables. Add the Parmesan cheese and stir to combine. Taste and add salt or more cheese to taste. Serve at room temperature or cold. Stores up to 4 days refrigerated.

Notes

Tortelloni is large tortellini that you can find in the refrigerated section. It's best for this salad because traditional tortellini is too small.

Using neutral oil in this pasta salad helps leftovers keep in the fridge: if you use only olive oil, it clumps up after about one day of storage. If you're not planning to have leftovers, you can use 100% olive oil.

In a rush? Substitute ¾ cup of Italian dressing or your purchased vinaigrette dressing of choice for the homemade sauce.

FRESH TOMATO SALAD

Prep Time: 10 minutes

Cook Time: 30 minutes

Ingredients

- 4–6 large ripe tomatoes, heirloom or multi-colored if possible

- 2 tbsp minced fresh herbs
- 2 tbsp extra-virgin olive oil
- 1 tbsp balsamic vinegar
- ¼ tsp flaky sea salt
- Fresh ground pepper

Instructions

1. Slice the tomatoes into wedges, leaving the seeds attached. Cut off any tricky parts of the core.
2. Mix all the ingredients in a bowl and stir gently to combine.
3. Cover and rest at room temperature for 30 minutes (or up to 2 hours) before serving.

BEST TOSSED SALAD

Ingredients

- 1/2 recipe Homemade Croutons
- One romaine heart (3 cups of chopped)
- 5 cups of mixed greens
- 1/4 small red onion
- 1 to 2 green onions (thinly sliced)
- 1/2 cucumber (1 cup of peeled and chopped)
- One carrot (shredded)
- Four radishes (thinly sliced and halved)
- ¼ cup of pepperoncini
- ¼ cup of sunflower seeds
- Sea salt, for garnish
- One of these dressings:
- Creamy Avocado Dressing
- Best Balsamic Vinaigrette
- Homemade Ranch Dressing
- Dijon Mustard Dressing

- Italian Dressing
- Blue Cheese Dressing
- Citrus Salad Dressing

Instructions

1. If you want to use them, make Homemade Croutons.
2. Wash the romaine and cut it up. If you need to, wash the greens. You can use any combination of gardens here. Every serving should have about 2 cups of greens.
3. Cut the red onion into thin slices. Cut the green onion into thin pieces.
4. Peel the cucumber and cut it up.
5. We used this Handheld Julienne Shredder to cut the carrot into thin strips.
6. Slice the radishes thinly and cut them in half.
7. Choose the dressing and make it (one of the above dressing recipes will do).
8. Mix the greens, the red onion, the green onion, the cucumber, the carrot, the radishes, and the pepperoncini. Sunflower seeds and croutons go on top, and dressing goes on top.

SQUASH SALAD

Prep Time: 10 minutes

Cook Time: 20 minutes

Ingredients

- One recipe Roasted Delicata Squash
- One large shallot
- 2 tbsp chopped pistachios
- 5 ounces baby mixed greens (about 5 cups)
- ⅓ cup of pomegranate seeds

- 2 tbsp roasted salted pepitas
- 2 ounces soft goat cheese (omit for vegan)
- Honey Mustard Dressing (use maple syrup for vegan)

Instructions

1. Cook the Roasted Delicata Squash. In total, this takes about 25 to 30 minutes. While the squash roasts, finish the rest of the prep work. Or, you can roast it ahead of time, put it in the fridge, and heat it in a 400-degree oven for 5 to 10 minutes until it's warm.
2. Make the dressing with honey and mustard.
3. Cut the shallot into thin slices. Chop the pistachios if you need to.
4. Put the greens on a plate to serve them. Top with roasted delicata squash, shallot, pistachios, pomegranate seeds, pepitas, and dollops of goat cheese. Drizzle with Honey Mustard Dressing, and then serve.

RADISH & GORGONZOLA SALAD

Ingredients

- 1/2 head green cabbage
- 1/2 head romaine lettuce
- 8 to 10 radishes
- Gorgonzola cheese crumbles
- One recipe Creamy Blue Cheese Dressing

Instructions

1. Chop the cabbage and the romaine lettuce into bite-sized pieces. Slice the radishes.
2. Make the Blue Cheese Dressing using Gorgonzola cheese.

3. Toss the vegetables and the desired amount of dressing. To serve, top with Gorgonzola crumbles and fresh ground pepper.

CUCUMBER SALAD

Ingredients

- 2 English cucumbers(1 3/4 to 2 pounds)
- 1/2 white onion, thinly sliced
- 1/2 red onion, thinly sliced
- 3 tbsp chopped fresh dill or 1 tsp dried dill
- ½ cup of white vinegar
- 1 tbsp water
- 2 tbsp granulated sugar
- 1 tsp kosher salt
- New ground black pepper, to taste

Instructions

1. Slice the cucumbers as thinly as you can. If you want, you can use a mandolin. Cut the onion into thin slices.
2. 2. Mix the white vinegar, water, sugar, salt, and pepper in a small bowl. Pour the mixture over the cucumbers and onions and mix it all up to ensure it covers everything evenly. You can serve it right away, but the vegetables will be softer if you put them in the fridge for an hour.
3. Stir again to make sure the dressing is well mixed. Then serve with a spoon with a hole in it. Keep in the fridge for up to 7 days.

Notes

English cucumbers don't have seeds and have fragile skin and mild flavor. They are worth looking for if you want to make this recipe. If you wish, you can use the same weight as regular cucumbers. Just make sure to slice them very thinly or peel them if the bitter taste of the skin bothers you.

FRENCH POTATO SALAD

Prep Time: 5 minutes

Cook Time: 30 minutes

Ingredients

- 3 pounds of baby red potatoes
- ¼ cup of minced shallot (about one large)
- ¼ cup of white wine vinegar
- 1 tsp kosher salt
- ¼ cup of capers, drained
- 1 tbsp fresh parsley
- 2 tbsp olive oil
- Fresh ground pepper

Instructions

1. Add 1 tbsp of kosher salt to a large pot of cold water. Bring to a boil, then add the whole potatoes. When it starts to boil, put an 8-minute timer on it. Cook until fork tender (taste test to check).
2. Chop the shallot up.
3. Drain the potatoes when they are done. When they are cool enough to touch, cut them into pieces that are easy to eat. Put the potatoes in a bowl and add the minced shallot, white wine vinegar, kosher salt, and 1/2 cup warm water. Mix everything gently. Let it sit for 5 minutes, stirring it gently every so often. As the potatoes sit there, the water will soak into them.

4. Add the capers, parsley, olive oil, and a few grinds of black pepper. Taste it and add more salt if you think it needs it. Serve at room temperature or warm.

GREEK SALAD

Ingredients

- Four large ripe tomatoes
- 1/2 large red onion
- Two large cucumbers
- 1 cup of Kalamata olives
- 4 ounces high-quality feta cheese: crumbled, cut into squares, or in a block (Greek feta, if you can find it!)
- 2 tbsp olive oil
- 1 tbsp red wine vinegar
- 1 tsp dried oregano
- 2 tbsp capers
- Kosher salt

Instructions

1. Cut the tomatoes into chunks and take them out and throw away the seeds. Put the tomatoes in a big bowl and sprinkle some kosher salt.
2. Cut the red onion into thin slices. Peel the cucumbers in strips, making a striped pattern with the peels (alternatively, remove the peel entirely). Cut the cucumbers in half and use a spoon to scoop out the seeds. Then, cut the cucumbers into pieces that are 12 inches long.
3. Mix the tomatoes, red onion, cucumbers, Kalamata olives, feta cheese crumbles, olive oil, and vinegar in a large bowl. Add the dried oregano and capers if you want to. Mix gently.

4. You can serve it right away, or you can let it sit at room temperature for a few minutes to let the flavors mix.

APPLE MANCHEGO SALAD

Ingredients

- Four firm tart apples (Jonathon, honey crisp, or Granny Smith)
- 1/2 lemon
- 4 ounces Manchego cheese
- ¼ cup of chopped chives
- 1 tbsp olive oil
- Two pinches of kosher salt

Instructions

1. Cut the apples into thin strips (slice them into slices, then lay the piece down and cut into long thin rectangles). Mix some fresh lemon juice with the apples.
2. Matchsticks are a good size for the cheese.
3. Cut the chives into thin slices.
4. Mix everything with olive oil and kosher salt. Serve right away.

EASY BRUSSELS SPROUT SALAD

Prep Time: 20 minutes

Yield: 6

Ingredients
For the salad

- 1 pound Brussels sprouts, enough for 4 cups of shredded (or 8 ounces shredded)

- 1 ½ cups of chopped escarole or other crunchy leafy greens, optional
- One large crisp tart red apple (like Honeycrisp)
- ½ cup of dried tart cherries
- ½ cup of almonds (Marcona almonds, if possible)
- ¼ tsp kosher salt
- One recipe for Dijon Mustard Dressing
- Feta cheese crumbles,

Instructions

1. Shred the Brussels sprouts: go to How to Shred Brussels Sprouts. Or, use a food processor slicing blade or mandoline to slice every shoot from top to end.
2. Prep the vegetables: Chop the escarole or other leafy green. Dice the apple.
3. Make the dressing: In a medium bowl, whisk together the Dijon mustard, white wine vinegar, maple syrup, and salt. Then whisk in the olive oil 1 tbsp at a time until a creamy dressing forms.
4. Assemble the salad: Mix all salad ingredients. Mix with ½ cup of the dressing (add more to taste, if desired). Top with feta crumbles, if using, and serve.

THE END

Made in the USA
Monee, IL
19 February 2023

28263560R00105